Our Glassrooms

Our Glassrooms

Perceptiveness and Its Implications for Transformational Leadership

Dhruva Trivedy

BEP BUSINESS EXPERT PRESS

Our Glassrooms: Perceptiveness and Its Implications for Transformational Leadership

Copyright © Business Expert Press, LLC, 2019.

First published in 2019 by
Business Expert Press, LLC
222 East 46th Street, New York, NY 10017
www.businessexpertpress.com

ISBN-13: 978-1-94944-364-6 (paperback)
ISBN-13: 978-1-94944-365-3 (e-book)

Business Expert Press Human Resource Management and Organizational Behavior Collection

Collection ISSN: 1946-5637 (print)
Collection ISSN: 1946-5645 (electronic)

Cover and interior design by Exeter Premedia Services Private Ltd., Chennai, India

First edition: 2019

10 9 8 7 6 5 4 3 2 1

Printed in the United States of America.

Let's not overlook our links with history as it helps us to anchor ourselves and know how we have evolved.

—Narendra Bhai Modi

Abstract

We have had various leadership attributes discussed across the world and most of them have been accepted, but this one attribute of perceptiveness has been overlooked, particularly in the context of transformational leadership. In this book the entire effort has been to focus on the significance of perceptiveness of an individual that takes one to formidable heights, to show its relevance in the most revered professions and more so in the corporate world. Individual personalities and their life stories have been depicted to highlight this experience. The style of managing the corporate has been most susceptible to change for the rapid growth in technology and changes in the physical and social environment. These leadership styles are prone to quick adaptation and perceptiveness is the one attribute that will show the way. Relevance of the attribute has been discussed with examples in different functional domains. The success stories of some organizations with futuristic vision have also been cited in the concluding part of the book.

Keywords

alertness; awareness; behavior; leadership; responsiveness; transformation; watchfulness

Contents

A Few Words About the Book

Mike H. Pandey

Futurist, Environmentalist and Film Maker

www.riverbankstudios.com

Evolution is the key to survival of any species.

Mankind has taken a quantum leap from the Stone age to the modern age of electronics, where humankind is pushing the boundaries of outer space.

Knowledge, adaptation and execution are crucial, but perceptiveness is the key catalyst, leading to transformation.

Such catalysts as always, play a role in leveraging the state of consciousness, comprehension and processing information.

Our Glassrooms, as the title suggests, is all about the transparency of the mind, to keep receiving information and registering them to be able to add to one's repository of knowledge—perceptiveness. This could be a pattern of behavior observed in certain persons or changing situations and responses to cope with them or even happenings and events with a foretold repercussion. The transparency to receive is complemented with a high degree of alertness, else the filtration process of the mind would let go of certain data that may prove relevant now or later. The author takes the reader through examples quoting biographies of certain luminaries in different fields—from writers to film-makers to teachers to corporate leaders. How each domain in a working organization needs to have perceptive human resources and how significantly relevant it is in today's volatile environment posing challenges to the transformational leader. The author has substantiated his stand with data collected through a survey. It is a reading which unveils that essential attribute of a human being, which would soon become indispensable for success, however, one may define the latter.

Success usually comes after years of experience but awareness, knowledge and wisdom help adaptation, enabling us to keep pace with the emerging challenges in our rapidly changing world. The book has the substance that not only motivates and inspires but also takes the reader on a journey at another level of transformation and insights, opening new doors and a new world.

Raghuram H. R.
Industrialist and Corporate Leader [MD, C.S. Aerotherm Pvt. Ltd.]
www.csaerotherm.org

What is it that shapes and drives a few individuals to achieve a high order of excellence in their chosen fields of human endeavor? Mankind has seen through ages, how a few rare men and women have made extraordinary contributions to society resulting in seminal changes. These famous personalities have undergone as much vicissitudes in life as much as, or sometimes even more than common folk. Yet they have scaled new heights and have become legends transcending generations and centuries.

Dhruva Trivedy in OUR GLASS ROOMS offers a fresh insight into the special trait, which these men and women possessed in abundant measure, that drove them toward excellence. In common parlance, we attribute the success of these people, to the qualities such as Inspiration, Perseverance, Passion, Inner drive and Inherent talent. They are true in varying degrees. Trivedy's in-depth study of the lives and work of some of the well-known legends such as Shivaji—the intrepid warrior, Sarvepalli Radhakirshnan—Teacher/Philospher and Statesman, Akira Kurosowa, Cecil De Mille and Satyajit Ray famous film makers and Qazi Nazrul Islam, the legendary poet of Bangladesh, has concluded that "Perceptiveness" is the single most important characteristic which has had an abiding presence in the lives and works of these men.

Trivedy has brought out with remarkable success different manifestations of the perceptive ability.

That Perceptiveness has universal and global dimensions is evident the way Akira Kurosowa deeply steeped in orient, cultural and social moorings could be sensitive to nuances of western societies with humanism as a common denominator. The sensitive nature of Nazrul Islam's persona was such that it embraced rich traditions of Sufism, Hinduism and folk tradition. Lesser mortals would have succumbed to the upheavals in life which Nazrul Islam faced and survived including severe financial stress, sick wife and loss of children in their early infanthood. Trivedy brings out a direct relationship between the deep understanding of themselves as these people on the one hand and their heightened awareness. He says and truly so, that a perceptive teacher can ignite a fire in his students only if he has the flame within himself. A deep understanding of his adversaries made Shivaji a brilliant strategist. Remarkable sensitivity of Kurosowa and Satyajit Ray made it possible for them to relate to their audiences.

Trivedy has also attempted to provide an empirical basis for his insightful analysis of biographical evidence. His survey focuses on eliciting responses of participants on their perceptive ability to respond to different situations in their daily lives. It is revealing that percentage of people with high degree of perceptiveness range from a high of 37 percent to a low of 19 percent. The fact that the percentage of population with perceptive ability is in minority, proves that this trait is a little hard to find. The book is eminently readable, in that it brings out hitherto unexplored factor of perceptiveness, which plays a crucial factor in shaping our lives, and more so in leadership roles.

Debi S. Saini, PhD
A renowned HR author and Emeritus Professor, IIM Ranchi,
MDI Gurgaon
http://sites.google.com/site/debissaini

The key aim of strategic human resource management interventions is altering the behavior of people in organizations, so as to be, in sync with customer expectations. Perception is an important driver of behavior. Trivedy's book builds useful perspectives understanding the perception and alertness dynamics in producing behaviors. It will help the reader in imbibing transformational leadership competencies as also people-centric behaviors.

Confessions

It took me good three years to ascertain as to how I should go about titling my work. Nothing was seemingly more apt than the title of the concept I wished to describe, notwithstanding how tedious it was. Well, contextually I must mention here that I saw the idea of citing historical events and personalities of fame as the only gateway of reaching people at large to explain my thoughts; and while I researched to prove my point, the discovery of the title didn't happen till today. I still remember that I woke up in my sleep to grope my way toward the washroom and as I switched on the lights, the flash occurred! Oh my! Can I deny His presence? "Glass Room" was what flashed, and I thought nothing could be more befitting, because the work describes that kind of mind, which is endowed with "open" receptivity from all directions and transparency. Having zeroed in on the title, I was pushed to see if it had been used for by someone else at another place. There you were! Simon Mawer, who had his book "The Glass Room" nominated for the Booker Prize in 2009, had beaten me to it! So, I decided on presenting it differently...after all it was something to do with ourselves...so why not "Our Glassrooms"?

That was for the title. Now the other challenge was the style of stating facts. Since illustrations were from biographies or historical facts, I was sure that the narrations would not be too captivating, unless one was keenly interested in understanding facts. I took a chance.

I chose happenings and characters, which were closer home. There were already enough of them that lit the west to limelight. The global renaissance drove me one step closer to kindle this motivation. Essentially one event or one character has been picked from Asia or more so from South Asia to illustrate the thought. This was not definitely to undermine the west, but perhaps only to underline that Asia too was a happening place in recent times and it bore enough testimony in admiration of the processes of the mind that this book wants to bring to the fore.

In 1955, I was introduced to Reverend Brother Ponies of the Irish Christian Brothers at St. Columba's School in New Delhi for an informal assessment if I could go to that school. My sister was a product of the neighboring school, Convent of Jesus & Mary and it was her ardent desire that I went to Columba's (as it is known in NCR now). While they were talking I watched the colorful panes of the arch that held the entrance, quite in awe and admiration. Brother Ponies noticed my behavior and I was admitted. That was how perceptiveness was valued even then!

The Parley

Here is a narrative from the leaves of history of medieval India or Bharat, as it is preferred to be called by many Indians now. The 13th century saw the consolidation of the Bahamani Sultanate in the Deccan region of India. In the subsequent years a cultural upheaval prevailed in the region with the *afaqis,* (settlers from the middle-east) and the *dakkhanis,* the original stock of courtiers becoming contestants to positions of power. To complicate this rivalry, Hindus were engaged as governors and more so as a strategy to have a populist control of the area. The handsome Shahaji Raje Bhosale was one such feudal lord working for the Nizam and Adil Shah of the Bahamani Sultanate, inherited from his father. Shahaji was extremely ambitious and soon established his own command initially by providing protection to the eight year old Nizam against the Mughals at the historic battle of Bhatvadi near Ahmednagar in 1624.

Shahaji Raje Bhosale

In 1622, Prince Khurram, who later came to be known as the Mughal Emperor Shah Jahan in the books of history, actually revolted against his father Jehangir, the Mughal Emperor and left him. Khurram was born of Manavati Baiji Lall, a Rajput Princess of Marwar, betrothed to Jehangir, who had also later married Noor Jehan the Empress of Sher Shah after he was killed in a battle with the Mughals. Noor Jehan had wrested more powers than the Emperor himself and was indulging in plotting ploys in the royal palace. Fearing abdication to the throne of Delhi, Khurram battled against his own father's army and when chased in defeat, took asylum with Shahaji Raje Bhonsle of Nizamshahi. To crush Shahaji and "rescue" Khurram, Jahangir had ordered his commander-in-chief Lashkar Khan to obliterate Nizamshahi. Accordingly, Lashkar Khan marched on to Ahmednagar with an army of 120,000 (1.2 lakhs). The Adilshahi Sultanate had also agreed to help the Mughals. The Adilshahi army numbered 80,000 men. Thus, a gigantic army of 200,000 (2 lakhs) strode into Ahmednagar. On the other hand, Shahaji had an army of 20,000 at his disposal. Shahaji had assigned 10,000 of these, the task of protecting and defending the Ahmednagar fort and town. The remaining 10,000 were with Shahaji. Something that he knew about the topography of the vicinity, the numbers that he commanded and the visualization of the humongous numbers that the enemy had brought in, altogether prompted Shahaji to use his "insightfulness."

Shahaji could envisage that such a huge army of the Mughals needed an enormous amount of food and water. Before the attack on Shahaji's forces, therefore, having travelled a long distance the Mughal and Adil forces were compelled to encamp on the banks of the Mehkari River, which flowed North to South. The river had a dam to conserve water, as Ahmednagar usually experienced shortage of water. However, this time, there had been ample rainfall. The river was flowing with abundant water and was full to the brim. Shahaji came up with a brilliant idea. With utmost care, cracks were developed in the dam, during the night itself, while the entire Mughal and Adil encampment was fast asleep. Suddenly, water started gushing out of the dam from each of the cracks. Mughals and Adils were clueless about what was happening. Within minutes a huge wall of irate water was running over the Mughals and Adils.

Everyone started running helter-skelter to save their lives. There was chaos and confusion. The whole encampment was flooded with water. Clothes, ration, arms, ammunition, cannons and horses—everything drowned. Dead elephants were seen floating in the water. Many were taken as prisoners. As many as 25 renowned, Mughal and Adil chiefs were imprisoned by Shahaji. It was a huge win for Shahaji, after which Shahaji became well known and became the famous Maharaja Shahaji Raje Bhosale, the father of Chhatrapati Shivaji Maharaj.

Chhatrapati Shivaji Raje Bhosale had inherited quite a few characteristics of his father including this very variety of "insightfulness," which was only chiseled and groomed by his wise mother Jijabai. The ballad of how Shivaji avenged the treacherous killing of his elder brother Sambhaji is well strewn in the columns of Maratha history. It would not be out of place to recount that story here to highlight this bit of "insightfulness" that Shivaji displayed.

Shivaji held a commendable position in parts of Maval, which was part of the Pune region. The Adilshahi court, however, wanted to curb his activities. The Adilshahs of Bijapur considered Shivaji's exploits at Torana, Kondana and Rajgadh as regional revolt. Afzal Khan, a renowned general of Bijapur who had previously killed Shivaji's brother Sambhaji, in a battle near Bangalore, was selected to crush this revolt and lead an assault against Shivaji. He started from Bijapur in January 1653. Shivaji had a small but agile army which served him to a great advantage with the guerrilla warfare in the mountainous terrains of Western Ghats or the Sahyadri Mountain Range. Afzal Khan knew this and wanted Shivaji to come out in the open and fight him in the plains where the large cavalry and the elephants in his armed forces gave him the advantage. Therefore, to incite Shivaji, he desecrated the temples of Bhavani in Tuljapur and the temples of Pandharpur, where Shivaji worshipped. Afzal Khan expected Shivaji to retort and attack him all agitated. Instead Shivaji sent Afzal Khan a letter saying how he did not want to confront him and instead wanted some kind of understanding between the two. He decided to meet him in the foot hills of Fort Pratapgadh. Afzal Khan was delighted at this opportunity as he found this as a chance for giving shape to his plot to kill Shivaji during this meeting. Shivaji had smelled treachery.

While Afzal Khan's forces consisted of 12,000 select Adilshahi cavalry, 10,000 infantry and 1,500 musketeers, accompanied by 85 elephants and 1,200 camels, his artillery consisted of 80 to 90 cannons. Complacence had set into the forces because of the long travel from Bijapur. Shivaji was accompanied with an army of merely 1,500. Shivaji Maharaj wore the chilkhat (chain-mail armor) under his clothes. Then he hid a dagger amongst the jewels he was wearing. Next he wore the wagh naukh (tiger claws) in his hands and wore 10 rings to cover them up. Shivaji entered the tent where Afzal Khan was waiting. Afzal Khan was a good foot and a half taller than Shivaji. "Shiva!" so saying Afzal Khan embraced Shivaji with the customary hug. He gripped Shivaji's neck under his left arm and struck him in the back with the dagger Afzal Khan had hidden. The dagger stuck against the chilkhat tearing the upper cloth garment. In retaliation Shivaji cut open Afzal Khan's stomach with his wagh naukh and the dagger. He fell out of the tent and was beheaded by one of Shivaji's guards. How Shivaji and his guards valiantly fought Afzal Khan's guards and how the 1,500 rode the mighty Adilshahi army was an outcome of skilled guerrilla warfare. If we read the episodes of Shivaji Maharaj, we would find many an act of this "insightfulness" combined with strategic warfare, just as we saw in Shahaji Bhonsle's victory.

Strategy is always best charted out with this "insightfulness." Strategy bereft of such "insightfulness" is mundane and can always be guessed by the opponent or the competitor. Learning about Shivaji, we are exposed to many instances of this kind of "insightfulness," which we in our parlance prefer to term as *perceptiveness*. Infinite research has gone to show that perceptiveness has not only been a key contributory factor in strategy formulation but also has had a significant quantum of role in building leadership, more so in contemporary leadership. Therefore it becomes imperative to take a closer look at this characteristic of ours.

Shivaji Maharaj gets at Afzal Khan

Trying to Define "Perceptiveness"

Introduction

For many years now, investigations have been carried out to discover and converge on the best workable leadership style. Irrespective of what style the leader adapts, there were certain attributes a successful leader always needed to display and the three essential and indispensable attributes according to me based on experience were none else than Perceptiveness, Empathy and Direction (Vision)!! As regards empathy and direction (which depend entirely on vision), enough of research has been conducted and there is enough material available on them, but not a sufficient quantum of work that I know of, has been found in the area of "perceptiveness," except those of David McClelland and Dr. Udai Pareek, however, in a different context. McClelland in his Human Motivation in the 1960s in a passing fashion mentioned about how important it was, to be perceptive, for a leader to be able to recognize the team-mates' orientation toward "achievement," "affiliation," and "power" as motivators. Udai Pareek defined "perceptiveness" in his book Training Instruments for HRD and OD as,

the ability to pick up verbal and non-verbal cues from others......
perceptiveness can be used appropriately or inappropriately. If a person is too conscious of others' feelings, he may inhibit his interactions. Similarly, a person who is too conscious of his own limitations will tend not to take risks. Effective perceptiveness can be increased by checking others' reactions to what is said. A person who does not do this (in other words, if he is not open) may become overly concerned about the cues he receives."

Students of behavioral psychology and even management may find this as an unexplored area for their research projects.

Some Dictionary Definitions

1. To know a person's real motives or intentions, such as to be a perceptive and an astute judge of character in order to size another up. The practice of assigning numbers to identify people is the probable source of this expression. Although one's "number" is a superficial designation, the expression connotes a deeper, more profound understanding of a person. *Have [someone's] number* dates from the mid-19th century and is current even in jails today.
2. To sense negative feelings of others toward one-self; to perceive subtle manifestations of hostility, often racial. This phrase, obviously based on the dual dimensions of physical and emotional coldness, originated in the jazz world.
3. To be capable of differentiating between two things; to be wise, not easily fooled or duped *or* to be able to differentiate between two things that are superficially alike but essentially dissimilar; to be discerning, to have a keen mind; to know the real thing from a counterfeit. (As early as the 14th century, the expression, "Lo, how they *feinen* [middle ages English to mean feigning] chalk for cheese. [John Gower, *Confessio Amantis* 1393]) The implication is that "cheese" is superior to or finer than "chalk." Thus, to be as "different as chalk and cheese" is to be as different as black and white, or day and night, even though chalk and cheese are similar in appearance. To go beyond appearances to try to perceive the true nature of something; not to be fooled by superficial glitter or plainness. This proverbial saying is attributed to the Roman Emperor, philosopher, and writer Marcus Aurelius (121–180): Look beneath the surface; let not the several quality of a thing or its worth escape thee. (*Meditations*)[1]
4. The thesaurus describes it as to be able to *look through a millstone*. To be discerning and sharp-sighted; to exercise keen powers of perception. A millstone is a large, opaque stone used in grinding grains. Therefore, the physically impossible challenge to see through a millstone can be met only figuratively by one of extraordinarily

---

[1] Meditations by Marcus Aurelius (translated into English in 1792 by Richard Graves).

keen perception. The expression appeared in print by the mid-16th century. "Your eyes are so sharp, that you cannot only look through a Millstone, but clean through the mind." (John Lyly, *Euphues and his England* 1680).

5. To understand the implications of another's words or actions; to see beyond the explicit and be sensitive to the implications of subtleties and nuances; to get the underlying message, whether intended or not, regardless of the words that couch it or the actions that convey it. The phrase was once literal; methods of cryptogrammic communication included the use of invisible ink for writing "between the lines" or the practice of relating the secret message in alternate lines. Thus, "reading between the lines" was crucial to receiving the message sent. Today the expression often refers to an ability to sense an author's tone or a person's ulterior motives. People who have not the shrewdness to read a little between the lines … are grievously misled. (*The Manchester Examiner* January 1886).

I have listed different interpretations earlier, only to explain the different perspectives. What emerges from all that has been stated is a real-time practical definition for the attribute.

Perceptiveness is that attribute of a person which wakes him up, to the presence of signals that are aroused from the senses of sight, smell, touch, taste or hearing and that may relate to human personalities, to situations or even to inanimate or animate objects (experienced). It is eventually these signals that help the perceptive person, as a behavioral symptom to pre-empt happenings or responses, which in turn help in accomplishing the solutions, well ahead of time.

We begin by looking at the leader who has a queue of challenges awaiting him, not because he is expected to possess the power of magic to perform the miracles and overcome the challenges, but we expect him to act or respond in an unprecedented way and address the issues in an innovative manner. When and in what circumstances do we think, he would be able to do it? Not when he would take his surroundings for granted and would build solutions around sheer analyses of facts that have occurred in the past. He would perhaps have to comprehend the situation and make his observations of the dynamics of the situation, understand as to who were the people involved and how they would respond to certain stimuli and whether also the environment could have an impact, and so on. What if he does not do this and relies on the traditional ways of addressing the challenges? He would end up dealing with people and situations for a temporary phase and/or the "solutions" he finds, that would boomerang with changing times and leave a feeling of disinterest or disgust. This is well illustrated by Noriaki Kano, Professor at Tokyo Rika University in his famous "Kano's Model of Customer Satisfaction," wherein one could deem the team-mates to be the "internal customers." Premonition comes by way of, or is an offshoot of that attribute, which we are calling "perceptiveness." The leader in this case uses his premonition (his foreboding) and strategizes accordingly; and his strategy is based on his experiences, his understanding of the people involved and that of the situation and his understanding of the concerned environment, again factors which rely entirely on his "perceptiveness." Figure 1 as follows describes the visual interpretation of "perceptiveness." Visual Thesaurus (http://visualthesaurus.com/) has made a key attempt in simplifying the concept through this illustration. Each aspect needs to be comprehended before one is able to grasp in totality, the attribute, we are trying to analyze and or to bring about clarity in conceptualizing.

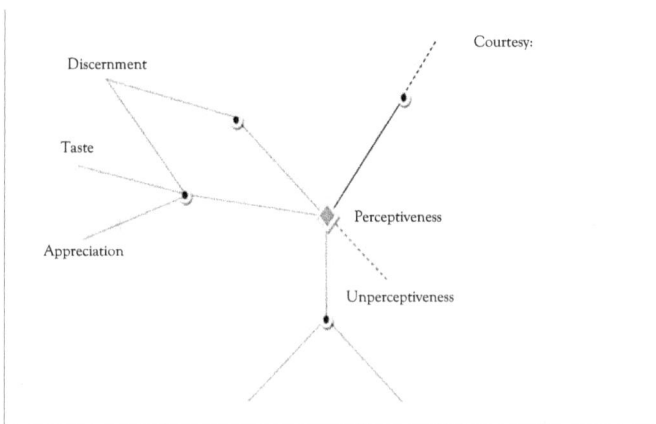

Figure 1 Visualising Perceptiveness

If we are to start comprehending the previous diagram, it would be convenient to take up one node at a time. In the clockwise direction if we try to explain each node, the very first node is that of "appreciation." Here appreciation would mean recognizing the existence of a fact, situation, event or a person or persons. When we go to the next node, "taste," it refers to the feel or the vibe that you collect from the fact, situation, event or a person or a group. All or some of your senses may be used to collect the information in both the aforementioned nodes covered. Now we come to the node of "discernment." This happens based on your previous experiences, skills and knowledge acquired, which assist your collection of information further from the fact, situation, event or a person or a group in question; and in order to explore the area of differentiation from your previous such experience, your collection of information further gets intensified [if you are positively curious to comprehend] through all your senses only to eventually augment your repository of experience, skill or knowledge. The lines in the diagram which do not lead you anywhere are efforts of the same strokes which go out in vain and remain unanswered. There's a certain section of your mind, which does not either comprehend or perceive the fact, situation, event or a person or a group.

The aforesaid description would continue to remain abstract, if an example is not provided here. There was an earthquake in the region recently, which devastated many lives, inhabitations and the surroundings. When it struck, in New Delhi, I was in my office on the second floor of the building, discussing an important project with my colleagues, absolutely focused and immersed in communicating certain points that were of valuable significance. I was in my revolving chair, behind my work table and my colleague with whom I was discussing had her seat next to mine, as the chairs in front were left vacant purposefully, for others to come and join the meeting that had just begun. Another colleague of mine was facing the wall and working on his system, with his back toward us. As we were talking, I found my chair had begun rocking and so were the furniture around. I stopped talking and within moments I declared that it was an earthquake, showing my colleague that the pictures on the wall were rocking too. The system screen that my other colleague was working on, was also swinging. "Yes!! Earthquake!" my colleague uttered. We were stunned and spoke little, as we heard the rumble underground.

My colleague wanted to leave the building and I assured her that it was an earthquake resistant construction and unless the intensity was vigorous, there was no point. We waited in silence without panicking and the ordeal was over within a span of a minute, while it seemed to us, that it was unending. Notwithstanding the intensity of the earthquake and the wreckage that followed, the example highlights the fact that even though we were in the midst of discussions, we identified that articles were visibly shaking *(appreciating)* and then collected the feel, an experience that there was a rumble, using our hearing sense and a forceful vibration, using our sense of equilibrium *(tasting)* and connected the two courses of action with the sense of previous experiences [use of knowledge and skills] of earthquakes, to be able to blurt *(discerning)*, "an earthquake!" To gather more information, we sought the help of the Internet and phone calls to establish the intensity of the quake. The mind, however, was reflecting on my experience of a 1962 earthquake[2] which had struck Delhi, shaken the power supplies out, developed cracks in the wall and had our doors pounding as if someone was trying to break through. Technology was not as advanced then and we all left the house we lived in, for the next one hour, to come back and discover the losses. The relevance of quoting this incident was that my mind was groping to find out more…if this earthquake was as severe or more. Even though the intensity may have been far greater and the epicenter much closer, the state of shock was less as the discerning ability through experience had compounded. Perceptiveness had begun playing its role.

---

[2] epicenter was Buin Zahara (Iran) http://en.wikipedia.org/wiki/1962_Buin_Zahra_earthquake

Brilliant Writers
Are Ingrained with
Perceptiveness

A blanket statement? Well, let's discover. Let's study a couple of examples.

Had the opportunity to make a short trip to the *Martin Wickra-masinghe* Museum at Galle. While plenty can be mentioned about the picturesque location of the museum on the banks of the Indian Ocean (the Koggalla reef), what is noteworthy was that it was also his residence which had been converted into a museum now. Looking at the collection of artifacts and going through his "Aspects of Sinhalese Culture" made a phenomenal revelation. He was fascinated by the culture of his island and worked tirelessly to both nurture and promote it. Martin became

Martin Wickramasinghe

Born the only son of Lamahewage Don Bastian Wickramasinghe and Magalle Balapitiya Liyanage Thochchohamy on the 29th of May 1891, in the village Malalgama. 1

By 1895, he had learnt the letters of the Sinhala Alphabet from Andiris Gurunanse. 2

Two years later he was sent to the village temple for traditional instructions. It is understood that he also learned the Devanagari script and could recite by memory long sections of the Hitopadesa 3

On his own, a year later he started exploring the marine life of the Koggala Reef situated about a quarter mile from his home 4

At the age of nine years Martin went to the Buonavista School in Galle to start his formal education. 5

After almost a year in school, in 1901, the family was struck with a tragedy, when Martin lost his father Don Bastian Wickramasinghe and due to financial hardships had to leave Buonavista School in 1902. 6

After almost a year in school, in 1901, the family was struck with a tragedy, when Martin lost his father Don Bastian Wickramasinghe and due to financial hardships had to leave Buonavista School in 1902. 7

It is understood that Martin was persuaded to write "Balopadeshaya" [Advice to Children] under the tutelage of the monk Koggala Deerananda Thero. Martin Wickramasinghe had confessed later that he was pressurised into writing this book, as a strategy of his mother and Rev. Deerananda to discipline him! 8

In 1904 Martin went to the Sinhala medium School in Ahangama. However as early as 1906, he left school at the age of 16 to work as book-keeper in one Carolis Silva's shop in Colombo again to quit and join a commissions agency run by John Silva in 1907. 9

In 1914, Martin published his first novel "Leela," but sadly he lost his mother before that. Meanwhile John Silva's agency was closed as an aftermath of the Sinhala-Muslim riots and Martin returned to Koggala. 10

In 1915 he again became a book-keeper in Cornelis Silva's shop in Batticaloa. 11

Nevertheless, 1916 saw the starting of his writing for the Sinhala Daily "Dinamina" under the pen name, "Hethu Vaadi" [The Rationalist]. This included a controversial series "Plants and Animals" and by 1920, Martin was elevated to the Editorial Staff of "Dinamina" the Sinhala national daily. 12

Five years later at the age of 35 years Martin was tied in wedlock with Kataluwe Balage Prema de Silva on the 30th of November, 1925   13

A year later the couple was blessed with a child, Susantha Manuwarna, after they shifted to stay at Mt. Lavinia. But this blessing was short-lived as Susantha died after 3 months, only to be blessed with son Sarath Kusum on 26th December, 1928 and again on July 16, 1929 with his second son Vasantha Kumara.   14

In the meanwhile in 1927 Martin had quit "Dinamina" to join "Lakmina". On February 4, 1931 Martin and his wife were blessed with daughter Rupa Malathie and the same year he became the Editor of the "Silumina" the Sunday weekly national newspaper.   15

While in 1932, Martin was blessed with another son Himansu Ranga, he was also appointed Editor of "Dinamina" the Sinhala national daily.   16

Three years later in 1935, Martin was gifted with another daughter Usha on September 20th. In four years to come in 1939 Martin built a house in Samudrasanna Road in Mt. Lavinia and this became his residence.   17

A year after this Martin had a daughter Unie. In just about a year from then, there was news that the Colonial Government took over Koggala and its adjoining villages, the place where Martin had spent his "exploratory" childhood, for a military air base.   18

In years to come he resigned from the post of Editor of "Dinamina". The family was becoming big and therefore in 1950 he sold his house in Mt. Lavinia and moved to Thimbirigasyaya closer to the heart of Colombo to enable his children to go to the university.   19

in 1953 he was awarded the Most Excellent Order of the British Empire [MBE] by her Majesty Queen Elizabeth in person and also appointed member of the Radio Broadcasting Commission.   20

In 1954, he was appointed to the National Languages Commission, Committe for making a glossary of scientific terms, but only to resign after 3 months.   21

In 1956 moved to Bandarawela, two hundred kilometres away in the east from Colombo. This place is well known across the world for its uniform pleasant weather throughout the year. He won the award for the best newspaper article for the year "The fall of the Brahmin Class".   22

In 1957, a visit to Southern India to study archaeological artefacts, inspired him to write his novel "Viragaya" which won the Don Pedric Award for the best novel of the year. However, he gave away the award money to create a scholarship fund for enabling a student from Karandeniya in southeast SriLanka to obtain a university education.   23

In the following years of 1958 and 1959 Martin visited the Soviet Union with his wife on the invitation of the Soviet Writers Union and toured many parts of China with his eldest daughter on the invitation of the Chinese Government, for the 10th Anniversary Celebrations of Peoples Republic of China, respectively.   24

In 1960 he was awarded the Honorary PhD by the Vidyodaya University, now known as the Sri Jayawardenepura University.   25

He returned to India a year later to participate in the centenary commemorative celebration of Rabindranath Tagore on the invitation of the Indian Government and in 1962, the Government of Sri Lanka handed over his birth place in Koggala with the house where he was born.   26

He now took up a house in Nawala, Rajagiriya, in Colombo, to stay. In 1963 Martin again visited Moscow and London and soon he was awarded the D.Lit by the University of Peradeniya [a suburb of Kandy].   27 self-aware through his surroundings, the landscapes of the sea, lake studded with little islands, the flora and fauna, the forested hinterland, and the changing patterns of life and culture of the villagers. From the age of five he traversed the alphabets of Sinhala, Devanagri and English and finally even gave up schooling, only to become a great scholar, philosopher and inspirational writer, gathering a sense of pride for Sri Lankans—no formal education in the early years of his life.

It would be worth looking at his personal history here, in a chronological manner. Events that need our attention have been highlighted in following text boxes, so that one can glance through and feel the impact, those events could have made in his life.

The following year was extremely eventful for Martin. He was bestowed the UNESCO Award for his book "The Rise of the Soviet Land," after he visited Havana, Cuba with his wife at the invitation of the Writer Congress of Cuba. He visited London again and Paris too on his return journey. Lester James Peries launched the film, "Gamperaliya" adapted from the works by Martin from his novel with the same name. The film won the prestigious "Golden Peacock" Award at the International Film Festival in New Delhi. The same year saw the D. Lit. awarded to him by Vidyalankara University (Kelaniya University). In 1968, Martin visited Cuba again on the invitation of the Cuban Government and in 1970, celebrations were held to commemorate his 80th Birthday organized by the Sri Lanka Writers Congress in Koggala and in many parts of the island. The same year the University of Colombo decided to award him another D. Lit.

The years that followed, saw him travelling [1972] as a guest of the Indian Government to Sanchi, Bauddhagaya, Gijjakuta, Nalanda and other regions where the Buddha trod. Two years later Martin received the first Presidential Award of Sri Lanka for Literature. He decided to donate the award money again, this time to the Minister of Cultural Affairs to initiate a scholarship. In his last few years Martin published "Bhava Tharanaya" [1975], a novel depicting the life and times of Prince Siddhartha, followed by a collection of essays [1976] Manawa Vidyawa ha Sinhala Sanskruthiya (Sinhalese Culture: Anthropological Perceptions) besides preparing two other books for publication, which were published posthumously by the M W Trust. Martin died a peaceful death on July 26, 1976, after a very brief illness.

(The graphic representation of the facts narrated earlier, is intended only to facilitate the reader to review them and make it easier to catalogue them.)

Having read this short biography, one is unmistakably led to the following inferences. (1) There was no structured and persistent form of early education that Martin Wickramasinghe had. (2) He exploited his perseverance to the hilt, in order to acquire knowledge, as he realized that he was in a socially handicapped situation. His learning of the basics of Sinhala coupled with his picking up the cues on the traditional instructions was to do with the basic culture of Sri Lanka. More than 70 percent of Sinhalese are Theravada Buddhists. Amongst Theravada Buddhists a smaller sect Amapura Nikaya emerged from the 19th-century social mobility of the Karava, Salagama, and Durava castes of the maritime provinces. Koggala was a maritime province and the instructions Martin received were from the Amapura Nikaya sect of the Theravada Buddhists. During these years it is remarkable to observe that Martin also acquired the knowledge of Devanagri script [used in Sanskrit, Hindi, Marathi, and Nepali] and learnt the Hitopadesa, a compilation in Sanskrit from the 11th or the 12th century from the times of the Pala Dynasty in Eastern India. Simultaneously, he also kept researching the Koggala reefs for its habitat and artifacts. Diverse activities and learning was the key to Martin's development in those years. (3) Alternating (research required on birth control in Sri Lanka) between the numerous efforts of seeking newer assignments and family commitments, we have found the family grow. All ethnic groups in Sri Lanka preserve clear distinctions in the roles of the sexes. Women are responsible for cooking, raising children, and taking care of housework. And therefore Martin could find time and well swap quickly between the growth in his vocation [you found him quitting jobs frequently] and the growth of his family. (4) Martin had a flair for writing and we discover this trait sufficiently well, from the fact that he stopped oscillating between vocations, once he could pen down his thoughts in chronicles such as the "Dinamina," the "Silumina" and the like. Rest of it was history. He rose from a newspaper columnist to not only a person of global eminence but also was the one, who founded a representation of the Sinhala civilization across the international borders. No wonder his abode has now been converted to a menagerie and we have a huge number of visitors, every day, only to get inspired to know more about the culture.

Now having substantiated the circumstantial support that subscribed to the maturity of this personality, it is comprehended well, that the tough terrain and lack of direction made Martin exploratory and simultaneously develop a desire to be aware of what was happening around him. Also he ventured into assignments that were not too close to his heart, but his "explorer" self was able to take the risks. He had to experience the learning that his vocation had to be one that he could "enjoy." His perceptiveness was chiseled to the core in the processes, which began from searching for artifacts on the Koggala reef to travelling across the world and find sync between other cultures and his own. Evidentially perceptiveness worked round the clock for him—creating an innate ability to alertly perceive and enhance his social awareness.

The other example that I cite is that of *Kazi Nazrul Islam*. Formed in the hot and tropical areas we discover a soil, which is rich in iron and aluminium and is largely rusty red, because of the presence of iron oxide and which develops because of intensive and long-lasting weathering of the underlying parent rock. Churulia, a village just about 15 km away from Asansol [West Bengal] on the banks of the Ajay river, proudly boasts of such a soil and also sees the remnants of a fort built by Raja Narottam, the last of the Panchet Rajas of Dhanbad [Jharkhand], in the form of a mound. This fort was captured by Sher Khan, the Afghan chieftain in the 16th century and the Mohammedan population grew under the Mohammedan rule. Most of the *zamindars* [landowners] in the area were Mohammedans and it is believed that their houses and mosques were built from the stones of the fort. This was the birthplace of Kazi Nazrul Islam and the resting place of his wife Pramila Devi.

He was born on May 24, 1899 to Kazi Fakir Ahmed, the caretaker of the local mosque and mausoleum, and his wife, Zahida Khatun. He was the second of their four children. Nazrul had two brothers, Kazi Saahibjaan and Kazi Ali Hussain, and a sister, Umme Kulsum. He began attending the maktab [a primary school *(Arabic)*] and madrassa [institution for Islamic instructions *(Arabic)*] run by the mosque and the dargah,

where he studied the Quran and other scriptures including Islamic philosophy and theology. After his father's untimely death in 1908, he was
nicknamed "Dukhu Mia" [man in grief] by the villagers because of the
hardships he faced in his early life. When he was 10, he started working
in his father's place as a caretaker to support his family, as well as assist-
ing teachers in school. Later he worked as a "muezzin" in the mosque.
The Muezzin's post is an important one, as he is the one responsible for
each call to prayer. The community depends on him for accurate prayer
schedules. Under normal circumstances, the grill of the madrassa and
the association with activities of the mosque would have yielded a person
of austerity and Islamic discipline, but to everyone's amazement, Nazrul was very much attracted to folk theatre, and enjoyed poetry, music
and dance. These interests prompted Nazrul to leave the madrassa and
join a travelling theatre troupe, a *leto* (travelling theatrical group) run by
his uncle Fazl e Karim. During his time in the troupe, the little Nazrul
learned acting and wrote songs and poems for plays and musicals. To
hone his skills, he began reading works of Bengali folklore as well as
Sanskrit works such as the Puranas. As a result, the 10 year old Nazrul
composed a good number of folk plays for the group, which included
"The Killing of Shakuni," "Kavi Kalidas (Poet Kalidas)" and "Data Karna
(Philanthropic Karna)."

Kazi Nazrul Islam

In 1910, he left the troupe to attend the Searsole Raj High School in Raniganj, a suburb of Asansol, where he came under influence of teacher, revolutionary and Jugantar [one of the two main secret revolutionary trends operating in Bengal for India's independence] activist Nibaran Chandra Ghatak, and initiated lifelong friendship with fellow author Sailajananda Mukhopadhyay, who was his classmate and then the Mathrun High English School at Burdwan, where he was taught by Kumudranjan Mallik, the principal of the school, who is known to be Nazrul's early coach and mentor and a great poet, himself (1883 to 1970). But soon he abandoned his studies due to an intense financial let down. To make both ends meet, Nazrul worked as a cook at the house of a railway guard besides selling tea at Asansol station and a job at a local bakery. It is at this time in his life, he also joined a group of kaviyals [a form of Bengali folk performance wherein folk poets *(kaviyals)* sing and perform]. During the year of 1914, Nazrul became familiar with a police inspector named Rafizullah, who gave him some financial assistance enabling him to join Darirampur School at Mymensingh, now in Bangladesh. But after finishing the 10th standard Nazrul did not appear for the matriculation pretest examination. He studied Bengali, Sanskrit, Arabic, Persian literature, and Hindustani classical music. In 1917, when he was 18, he joined the British Indian Army as a soldier and served there for three years, rising to the rank of Battalion Quarter Master (Havildar). As part of the 49th Bengal Regiment, he was posted to the cantonment in Karachi, now in the Sindh Province of Pakistan. During his stay at Karachi, Nazrul subscribed to some of the notable literary journals published from Kolkata like *Prabasi, Indiabarsa, Indiai, Manasi, Sahitya Patrika.* Besides these journals, he extensively read the works of Rabindranath and Sarat Chandra Chatterjee. In 1919, he published his first piece, "The Autobiography of a Delinquent" or "Saogat," while serving in the army. He took a liking for Persian poetry, as he also learned to read Persian poetry from the regiment's moulvi [Islamic priest], and practiced music as well. It was at Karachi cantonment that Nazrul's literary works started to get noticed. The May–July editions of the "Bangiya Mussalman Sahitya Samiti" [**Bengali Muslim Literary Journalistic Society**] published his prose work "Life of a Vagabond."

Nazrul left the army in March 1920 because the Bangali Platoon was dissolved and joined the "Bangiya Mussalman Sahitya Samiti" where he wrote his first poem "Bandhan-hara" or "Freedom from bondage." In 1921, he got engaged to Nargis [Sayyida Khatun (alias Nargis Ashar Khanom)], the niece of a well-known Muslim publisher, Ali Akbar Khan, in Daulatpur, Comilla, now Bangladesh. On the day of his wedding, he walked away from the ceremony upon hearing an unreasonable condition of Ali Akbar Khan. The same year he met a young Hindu woman, Pramila Devi [Ashalota Shengupta from Kolkata] on his visit to Comilla. They fell in love and he married her three years later in 1924. But before that in 1922, he wrote his poem titled "Bidrohi" which was published in "Bijli" (Thunder) magazine. The poem described a rebel passionate about his cause and received praises from people belonging to different classes of the society and therefore brought him to fame. In the same year, his political poem "Anondomoyeer Agomone" appeared in the magazine "Dhumketu" which he had started publishing. This led to his arrest during a police raid at the magazine's office. While imprisoned, he composed a large number of poems and songs until his release in December 1923, much to the agony of the British regime. Eventually, he became a critic of the "Khilafat" struggle and the Indian National Congress for not bargaining political independence from the British Empire. He also motivated people to fight against the British and organized the "Sramik Praja Swaraj Dal." In 1924, Nazrul was blessed with a son Krishna Mohammad, who however did not survive to see the light of the day. In 1925, he became a member of the Bengal Provincial Congress Committee. [It might be worthwhile to remember that with all these events in his life so far, at this time he was merely 26.] Toward the end of the same year he participated in the formation of the "Mojur Shoraj Party" (Labour Independence Party), an organ of "Bharotiyo Jatiyo Mohashomiti" (Greater India National Association). On 16th June, 1925, at the death of Chittaranjan Das, he wrote and published "Chittonama." In December 25 under Nazrul's directorship, the newspaper of Shoraj Party, Langol, started. The same year his book of poetry collection "Puber Hawa" [Eastern Wind] and the story "Rikter Bedon" [The agony of the Destitute] were published.

From 1926 onwards, he started writing poetry and songs for the weaker sections of the society. He wrote one of his most famous poems titled "Daridro" ("Pain or Poverty") which received appreciation from the classes as well as the masses. On August 12, 1926, Langol changed its name to "Gonobani" [People's voice]. His book of poetry "Shorbohara" [Destitute], and prose-work "Durdiner Jatri" [voyager of hard times] appeared at about the same time. From 1926 to 1928 the poet resided in Krishna Nagar and in 1926 another son of the poet, Bulbul, was born. That year he published "Jhinge phul." In 1926, Nazrul unsuccessfully contested for the Central Parliament. While residing in Krishna Nagar, his novel "Mrittu Khudha" was published. At the provincial conference in Krishna Nagar, he sang his famous song "Kandari Hushiyar." In 1927, Nazrul inaugurated the first convention of Muslim Shahitto Shomaj [Muslim Literary Society] in Dhaka. During that same year his books of poetry "Foni Monosha" and "Shindhu-Hindol" and the novel "Badhon-hara" were published. Nazrul's mother died in 1928, and the same year, "Jinjir" (chain), poetry collection "Shonchita" and Lyric collection "Bul-bul" (1st vol.) were published. One of his biggest works in the industry was writing songs and directing music for a bioepic play named "Siraj-ud-Daula" was also in the same year. On 15th December 1929, Nazrul was given a reception on behalf of the nation at the Albert Hall in Cal-cutta. Acharya Prafulla Chandra Roy, the famous scientist, presided at that meeting. The chairman of the reception committee was S. Wajed Ali and the main speaker was Netaji Subhash Chandra Bose. In early 1929, he was honored by the Bulbul Society of Chittagong. During the same year he presided at the meeting on the occasion of founding the Chit-tagong Muslim Education Society. Also, his "Chokrobak," "Shondhay," "Chokher Chatok," and "Chondro Bindu" were published.

In 1930, his book "Proloyshikha" was banned and confiscated under the accusation of sedition. He was sent to prison for six months. He was released as a part of a pact between Gandhi and Irwin. The same year his infant son, Bulbul, passed away, when he succumbed to the dreaded smallpox. While at the bedside of his sick child, he translated some works of Hafiz. His other two younger sons' were Kazi Shabyashachi Islam and Kazi Anirudhdha Islam. *The younger one died in 1974 even before Nazrul died and the older one in 1978—not long after the poet himself passed away. These two sons had made their own unique and remarkable contribution in recitation and the guitar, respectively.* In 1931, his lyric-collection "Shur

Saki," story "Sheuli Mala," novel "Kuhelika" and musical drama "Aleya" were published. The same year he joined the film and theatre industry. He directed a film, "Dhupchaya" and also acted in it. During November 5 through 6, 1932 he presided at the Bangiyo Muslim Torun Sham-melan [Bengal Muslim Youth Conference] at the theater hall in Sirajganj. His works "Zulfiqar" and "Bonogiti" were published. In 1933 "Kabyo Ampara" (poetical translation of the 30th segment of the Qur'an) and "Gul-Baghicha" lyric collection were published. In 1933, he also published a collection of essays entitled "Modern World Literature" which had different themes and styles of literature. He also published 800 songs based on classical ragas, kirtans and patriotic songs in 10 volumes. In 1934 while his works "Giti-Shotodol" and "Ganer Mala" were published, he also got involved in the Indian theatre and motion pictures and debuted in a movie based on the famous theatre promoter of those days, Girish Chandra's story called "Bhakta Dhruva." In 1936, he presided over the Muslim Students Convention in Faridpur District. In 1938, he wrote two film scripts: "Biddapoti" [play about the famous bard Vidyapati of Mithila] and "Shapure" [the snake-charmer] (Directed by Debokikumar Bose). He gave the presiding speech at the inaugural meeting of Jono Sha-hitto Shangshad. That year his poetry work "Nirjhor" was also published, though it did not get lot of publicity. He also published two opera script: "Shat Bhai Chompa" and "Putuler Biye." On 10th December 1939, he presided over the memorial meeting at the death of Ustad Jamiruddin Khan, the famous Thumri singer. It is noteworthy that he was also a mas-ter of Nazrul's Thumri genre. In 1939, also he started working for the Calcutta radio and produced music such as "Haramoni" and "Navara-ga-malika." In 1940, Pramilla the wife of the poet was affected by tuber-culosis. Also, during April 5 through 6, 1940 he gave the presiding speech at the silver jubilee of Bengal Muslim Literary Society held at the Muslim Institute of Calcutta. In 1940, he presided over the Eid Conference of the Bengal Muslim Literary Society. The same year he spoke at the opening of the "Shiraji Public Library and Free Reading Room" in Calcutta. On 23rd December, he again spoke at the Muslim Institute of Calcutta. In 1941, he accepted the chief editorship of republished Daily Nabajug run by his friend A.K. Fazlul Huq, who also assured him of clearing Nazrul's debts. Nazrul had been raising money for his wife's and his own illness, but sooner than later Huq started dragging his feet and it was at this time that the famous Dr. Shyama Prasad Mookerjee helped him out financially and sent him to Madhupur, where the latter had a house. Nazrul stayed there with his wife on the banks of the Ganga and started recovering. But, in 1941, he was shaken by the death of Rabindranath Tagore and within months, he himself fell seriously ill.

On 16th March, 1942, he presided at the 4th literary conference of Bongaon, which now lies as a border town on the India side, close to Bangladesh. Nazrul did not want to attend the Bongaon Literary Conference. But to understand Nazrul's mystic philosophy this address Modhurom (Delightful) is significant. On request from the subdivision magistrate Mizanur Rahman who took the chance in the poverty-stricken condition of the poet, Nazrul agreed to preside over the conference. On May 25, 1941 his 43rd birthday was celebrated and presided by Bengal's one of the most revered poets Jyotindramohan Bagchi. On 10th July, 1942 Nazrul was detected to be in the grip of an unknown disease, losing his voice and memory, possibly the "Pick's" disease. Eventually, his mental dysfunction intensified and he was admitted to a mental asylum in 1942. In 1945, Calcutta University honored him with "Jagottarini" gold medal. His "Notun Chand" [Crescent] was published. In 1952, a Society was established, known as the Nazrul Treatment Society, was formed and was spearheaded by Dr. Shyamaprasad Mookerjee. On 10th May, 1953 this very Society sent him and his wife to London for better treatment. However, after an unsuccessful attempt toward their treatment in London as well as in Vienna [considered to be a medical hub in those days] they returned home on 15th December, as their conditions did not improve. Although in 1955 his poetry collection "Shonchoyon" was published and later in 1957 his incomplete poetry-biography of the Prophet Muhammad (s) "Moru Bhashkor" was published from Calcutta, Nazrul kept being unwell. In 1958, "Shesh Saogat" was published and in 1959 "Rubaiyyat-e-Omar Khayyam" was published.

In 1960, the India Government honored him with the title of "Padma Bhushan." The same year "Jhor" (storm) was published. On 30th June 1962 his wife Promila Nazrul passed away and she was buried at Nazrul's birthplace Churulia, as already said earlier. On 24th May 1972 on a special invitation of the Government of Bangladesh the poet and his family were moved to Dhaka. Honored as the state guests, they were kept at a special residence at Dhanmondi Road. Special arrangements were made for his treatments, but to no avail. In 1974, Dhaka University honored the poet for his unparalleled literary contribution by conferring on him honorary doctorate degree. In 1975, he was transferred to P. G. Hospital in Dhaka. In January 1976, he was formally honored by the Government of Bangladesh by offering him the citizenship of the country. Later on 21st February, he was conferred the title of "national poet" and awarded the "Ekushey Padak" [gold medal] by the Government of Bangladesh. On May 24, 1976 he was honored by the Bangladesh Army with the Army Crest. On 29th August, 1976 (10:10 a.m.; 2nd Ramadan; 12th Bhadra, 1383) however, he breathed his last at the P. G. Hospital. The same day his funeral took place, when along with the President, millions of grief-stricken people of all backgrounds joined and with national honor he was buried at the courtyard of the Dhaka University Mosque.

Dr. Phyllis Herman, Chair, Department of Religious Studies, California State University, Northridge spoke thus in the year 2006 at the Nazrul Conference at the University of Connecticut,

When I began to study Nazrul, I found that he was also taken with the use of goddesses in India and yet he was a Muslim! I could not believe that I had found a new source for my work and from the national poet of Bangladesh.... Nazrul was very much from Bengal: he was drenched in a rich tradition of Hinduism, Sufism, folk tradition and the absolutely integral roles of religion in politics. His images in poetry, plays, essays, and music reflect a man who discarded nothing that would enrich the ideals he was trying to promote. In Nazrul's writing, he speaks of the sort of egalitarian melting pot of ideas from which he drew: I sing of equality in which dissolves all the barriers and estrangements, which is united Hindus, Buddhists Muslims, Christians. I sing of equality. His work reflects this and no more so than when he speaks of the Hindu goddesses....

The idea of quoting this piece of Dr. Herman's speech is to emphatically highlight the transition of Nazrul, from the poet to the rebel to the spiritual without setting boundaries for himself and remaining confined to a set of religious or national norms. Much to the agony of many stalwarts who adhered to the flow of the mainstream, Nazrul moved laterally on a bandwidth much larger than could have been comprehended by the intellectuals of those times. The first perspective that we may proactively observe is that he transitioned from the role of a muezzin in the mosque to an actor to a soldier in the army and eventually to a poet and writer, which shot him to fame. The many roles that he adapted only augmented his disposition toward perceptiveness. Nazrul was also a very emotional being. Therefore, on the other hand, as a second perspective, analytically speaking, his perceptiveness only enhanced his sensitivities toward the vicissitudes of life that he journeyed through. His constant endeavors to come out of his financial stress added to his woes of a sick wife, losing his children in their early infanthood, the feeling of having been ruined with the passing away of his confidant Rabindranath Tagore and above all the nation divided on the basis of religion. Nazrul stood shattered between what he idealized and the events in his life. All along the financial crisis was aggravated with eminently placed personalities letting him down after having promised financial assistance. The emotional Nazrul succumbed to the "Pick's Disease," a rare neurodegenerative disease that causes progressive destruction of nerve cells in the brain. It would not be wrong to suggest that unbalanced nutritive inputs which he had, because of his poverty, was only a physical cause. Nonetheless his emotional sensitivities to the constant trauma that he confronted, as a result of his being extremely perceptive to situations and people around him was equally responsible for the sickness. In effect however, the positive imprint left behind in this world by Nazrul, because of perceptive writings and spiritual approach toward humanity, transcending ritualistic norms and mores of the Society is undoubtedly, a hallmark in the subcontinent.

Both the writers, we see here, in this chapter, are examples of illustrious and discontented personalities who kept assimilating different virtues and exposure, while moving through different vocations, until the one found that quenched their passion. Ideals in life were to serve the humanity in whatever little way each one could. Both were intolerant toward fragmentation in Society based on religion, color and creed and therefore kept acquiring the essence of teachings in other their own traditional religious beliefs. They wished to traverse across religions and sections of society and redeem it from the shackles that were uselessly perpetuated by mankind.

"Perceptiveness is pronouncedly reflected when Martin Wickramasinghe in "Budusamaya ha samaja darsanaya" discusses the compatibility between Buddhism and Marxism," writes H.L. Seneviratne in his book, Work of Kings. Professor K.N.O. Dharmadasa's concluding essay in the book "From the Cradle—Glimpses of Sri Lankan Folk Culture" describes his perceptiveness through his creative and intellectual evolution—journalist, essayist, novelist, literary critic and pioneer popularizer of science. No contemporary Sinhala writer ever matched the variety of his interests and achievements. A strong social conscience always underpinned his writings.

While the famous singer of Bangladesh, Fahmida Nabi states that maturity and perceptiveness of Nazrul's philosophy is indispensable while working on his songs, Professors Mohammad Tajuddin and Md. Nazmul Huda of the University of Chittagong write that Nazrul's perceptiveness dealt with a variety of subjects in depth—self, love, body and soul, human dignity, democracy, equality, universal brotherhood and oneness of God—separately in different poems with different names.

The generalizations made earlier are not based on the biographies of only two handpicked writers of Southern Asia. Similar trends are seen in the lives of writers of the west. *Ernest Hemingway*, the Nobel Prize winner, for instance is seen as one of the great American 20th century novelists and is known for works like A Farewell to Arms and The Old Man and the Sea. From a newspaper columnist to a driver in the Word War 1 to a novelist, Hemingway wavered from the role of a journalist to a novelist. Surviving the war injuries, a plane crash in Africa and a series of unsuccessful marriages, Hemingway ran into depression, for his body and will were betraying his dreams. He had also become addicted to alcohol and drinks. Hemingway committed suicide and succumbed to his depression. What needs to be understood here is that he had not found his passion in his relationships, while he continued to write the greatest of novels. His perceptiveness was unquestionable.

Ernest Hemingway

It didn't fail him till his end came. But he carried it too far. Reverting to Udai Pareek in this context, we find that there's so much weight in his proclamation (Chapter 2), … "A person who does not… check others' reactions to what is said (or done)….may become overly concerned about the cues he receives." Hemingway was a victim of such a concern.[3]

---

[3] Training Instruments by Udai Pareek. Chapter 2. Published by McGraw Hill Education.

What About Teachers?

The scientist or an artist is equally perceptive; else they would not ever have sized up assessing a need or a context for research or a piece to create. But what pulls them away generally is the focus required in value adding to the work and how presentable, it would be. This is a very generic statement though, and we do have scientists of the caliber of Jagadish Chandra Bose, who turned out to be a polymath—physicist, biologist, biophysicist, botanist, archaeologist, as well as an early writer of science fiction. Couldn't have been what he was, if he wasn't perceptive. Likewise, we had Raja Ravi Varma, the painter from Kerala who travelled across the country for his choice of subjects and recalled his traditional Sanskrit learning, his Thanjavur training and also the training he acknowledged from the Dutch oil painter Theodor Jenson. Anchored and patronized by the Travancore Maharaja, the Maharaja of Vadodara and the Maharaja of Mysore, Ravi Varma was "sensitized" to a variety of subcultures, which reflected in his work. His dabbling with the press and coming close to the then freedom fighters added another dimension to his perspective. His family members were also involved either as subjects or as promoters because he was perceptive to their needs.

I have preferred talking about teachers, because unlike the previous chapter where I have dealt with writers, who go with the flow of events and their perceptiveness toward them, in vocations such as that of a teacher, perceptiveness is a dire necessity in contextual times for every moment of delivery. And I include trainers in this category.

Please see the following diagram, which pictorially depicts the role of perceptiveness in the performance of a teacher.

If we are to scrutinize this illustration carefully, we find that the underlying and all-pervasive feature of the profession, like all others, is *passion*. The straight line on top depicts the essence of passion in every communication made by the teacher, whatever the interface—whether it be students or be it the information-world. It's only the prevalence of passion that will send through the sense of involvement in each performer.

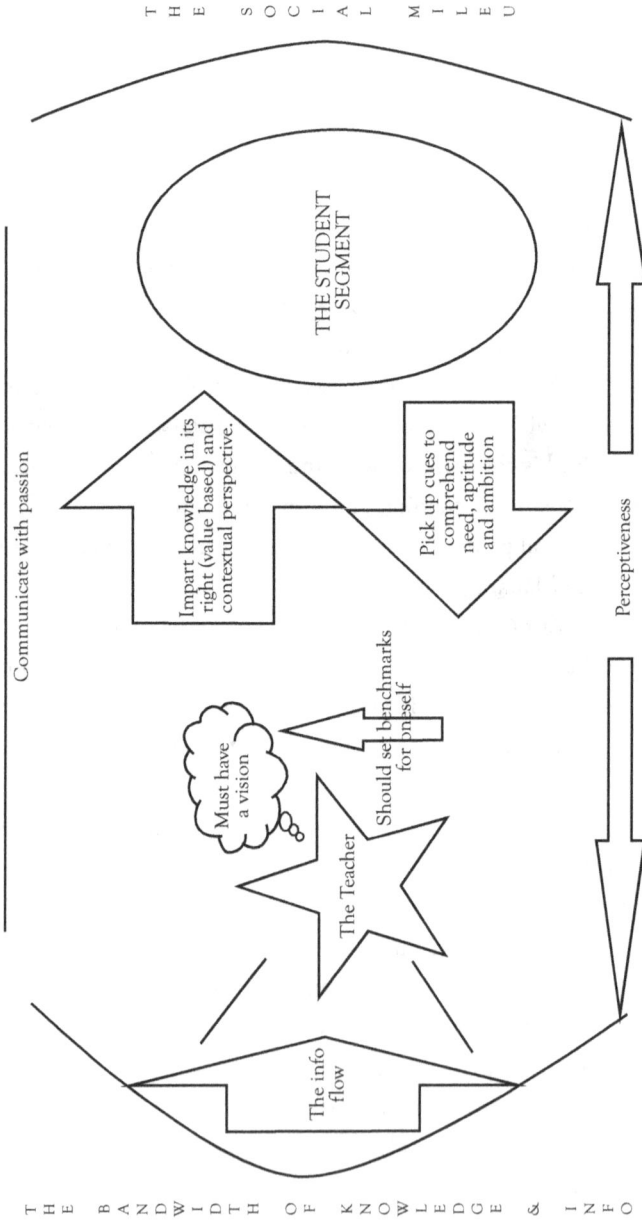

THE SOCIAL MILIEU

THE STUDENT SEGMENT

Communicate with passion

Impart knowledge in its right (value based) and contextual perspective.

Pick up cues to comprehend need, aptitude and ambition

Perceptiveness

Must have a vision

Should set benchmarks for oneself

The Teacher

The info flow

THE BANDWIDTH OF THE KNOWLEDGE & INFO

Figure 2 Perceptiveness in teachers

Else both the source of information and the audience would get to sense the smallest presence of apathy, which in turn would escalate with time and numbers and eventually go to ruin the performance.

Now we examine as to why perceptiveness becomes the quintessential feature of this profession. O*NET OnLine, which partners the American Job Center* Network, visibly allocates "social perceptiveness" as a critical skill required for educational administrators and counselors. Without idealizing the previous fact, let us accept that the information flow in today's context is unfathomable and seamless with the presence of the Internet, print and electronic media and the churning out of books in much larger volumes than it ever happened before. It depends on the teacher, therefore as to what he should access, how much should he filter and what portions could be registered as relevant knowledge. At the same time, it is significantly true that the teacher has to have admittance to all the information available. The teacher is not sensitized to deliver if this part of his homework has not been done, even if he or she may have the syllabi and the course material on his or her finger-tips. The findings of contemporary research are available to the teachers to add value to the syllabus and make the subject more interesting than ever. The interest generated in fresh or topical events is much more than what has happened in the past and if such events add value to the context or the concept, the excitement is much more. For instance, highlighting a comparison drawn out in the beliefs of Stephen Hawking (a contemporary physicist) and that of Sir Isaac Newton would invariably catch more attention with the student. Therefore, the use of the knowledge acquired on an ongoing basis also has to catch the attention of the teacher. This brings us to the second interface of the teacher. But before we start discussing that, it is imperative that we understand as to what would tutor the teachers' actions in using such knowledge.

What would be the tools that would not only help them to utilize the knowledge, but also to shortlist the information that needs to be transformed into knowledge (a) for immediate transference to the audience and (b) for the repository?

(a) Clear Vision

As late as 2009, Karen Hammerness from the Brandeis University, Waltham, USA has completed her work titled "The Relationship between Teacher Education Program Visions and Teacher's Visions," which simply goes to emphasize the vision of the teacher and its significance in the framework of teaching. According to me the teacher should have a career vision separated from an achievement vision and should lay down the foundation stone for the latter prioritizing over her "career vision." The achievement vision should spell out what best as a teacher one could deliver and eventually get into a mentoring syndrome—the guiding philosophy being the *"Guru Shishya Parampara."*

(b) Benchmark

They should fix timelines with each batch or batches of students and impart the value-add within that timeline. The value-add is a step closer to the vision in terms of information, knowledge and delivery including its strategy and method. That would mean that the content would be communicated in a manner most appropriate, left to the assessment of the teacher. This also means that the teacher should be adept in the state of the art styles of pedagogy, because only then can the teacher keep the interest of the audience in place and continue to have the latter energized to learn. The value adds need to persist with every benchmark and help the teacher-student team journey on a spiral reaching closer to the vision every time.

Now the second interface. This requires a regular count of perceptiveness. Although the alertness and social awareness does not have to wander far and wide as in the first interface, it has to be exercised day in and day out, watching events (including personal and familial), responses to behavior and situations and the traditions and norms that are being adhered to since birth. Empathy with the audience and its individual members is the key. This would set the platform to bringing in cues, even when you have not made a deliberate move to acquire them. Not to make the mistake of ignoring the information not required at that time. On the contrary they should be carefully catalogued in the repository of the mind. This has a dual advantage. The teacher is able to communicate and transfer the "knowledge" in the desired perspective and more effectively for certain. The second gain that the teacher derives is that he or she is better off learning what the needs of the students are, their likes and dislikes, aptitudes and ambitions. It would provide the teacher the occasion to discover whether the ambitions were in sync with the aptitudes, and a great podium to guide the students to achieve symmetry between what they cherish and what they should work for. The teacher has to assume the role of a mentor.

In order to illustrate, let us see in real life how an ideal teacher has set himself as a role-model. One of the greatest teachers in this part of the world was Dr. Sarvepalli Radhakrishnan, who subsequently became the first Vice President of India and the second President. Fundamentally, Dr. Radhakrishnan was a teacher and which is why the whole of India celebrates his birthday as "Teachers' Day." Dr. Sunil Kumar Singh, Associate Professor, Faculty of Education, B.H.U. wrote in his paper, "The Great Teacher Dr. Sarvepalli Radhakrishnan: Life, Vision and Actions," the following.

His actions as a Teacher began in 1909 and continued even after completion of Teachers Training in 1910. Once he was asked by his student if he had been abroad for education. He replied, no but I will go there to teach. Such was his determination. He was very friendly with his students. At Mysore while giving tutorials to students at his residence, he used to receive students himself, offer tea and used to see off them to door. He used to shake hands with each of them. He was given a unique farewell by students when he left for Calcutta University. His carriage during departure was pulled by students and not by horses and the entire platform was full of cries, "Radhakrishnan ki jai" [Victory to Radhakrishnan].

Even in Calcutta University he took active part in bodies of the university. He was very popular among teachers and students. He was an eloquent speaker. As narrated by a student, once a foreign scholar spoke for 50 min on Greek Philosophy in Calcutta but audience could not understand him. Dr. Radhakrishnan spoke the gist within 10 min and audience was satisfied. As Vice-Chancellor of B.H.U. he solved many problems and even saved the university from atrocities of British forces. He also ensured its educational development. He was not only a teacher for his students but also for his colleagues and diplomats too. According to him a teacher should have openness of mind. He said that, "the True Teacher helps us to deepen our insight, not alter our view. He gives us a better access to our own scriptures." Further according to him:

The true teachers help us to think for ourselves in the new situations which arise. We would be unworthy disciples if we do not question and criticize them. They try to widen our knowledge and help us to see clearly. The true teacher is like Krsna in the Bhagavadgita, who advises Arjuna to think for himself and do as he chooses yatha icchasi tatha kuru. (Banerjee 1991, p. 15)

He was a great teacher because he reinterpreted the past to weave something new for us in all spheres of life particularly teaching, philosophy, politics and religion. As he himself quoted Confucius saying that, "He who by re-animating the Old can gain knowledge of the New is fit to be a teacher."

Further, Dr. Santosh Kumar Behera, Asst. Professor, Dept. of Education, Sidho-Kanho-Birsha University, Purulia, West Bengal has added and compiled in his "Educational Thoughts of Dr. Sarvapalli Radhakrishnan" all the ideas of Dr. Radhakrishnan on what an ideal framework of education needs to be. What I have reproduced here are the excerpts that are most relevant, in terms of the perceptiveness of a teacher.

According to Radhakrishnan a true teacher always helps us to think for ourselves in the new situations which arise. They try to widen our knowledge and help us to see clearly. The Indian education system did not change much from what he cautioned 67 years ago.

Dr. Sarvepalli Radhakrishnan

The process of education becomes dull and boring if we are unable to interest the live minds of the students. What they learn unwillingly becomes dead knowledge which is worse than ignorance. Learning is an activity of thought. It is not stuffing the mind with facts. We must be able to use what we learn, test it, throw it into fresh combinations. It must become vibrant with power, radiant with light. (First University Education Commission Report 1948)

He believed that,

A good teacher must know how to arouse the interest of the pupil in the field of study for which he is responsible. He must himself be a master in the field of study and be in touch with the latest developments in the subjects, he must himself be a fellow traveler in the exciting pursuit of knowledge.

He says,

A teacher who has attained the goal may help the aspiring soul. Truth was not only to be demonstrated but also communicated. It is relatively easy to demonstrate, a trust but it can be communicated only by one who has thought, willed and felt the truth. Only a teacher can give it with his concrete quality. He that has must be a proper teacher who embodies truth and tradition, only those who have the flame in them can stir the five in others.

Teachers as Removers of Spiritual Blindness: Guru is the combination of two words—"Gu" means darkness and "ru" means to remove. In our country we look upon teachers as "gurus," and "acharyas," which indicates "achar" or conduct that is exemplary or good. Teachers must love the good and detest the bad. "Andhakar" [Darkness] is not merely intellectual ignorance but spiritual blindness as well. One who is able to remove that kind of spiritual blindness is called a "guru."

Teachers–Reservoirs of New Spirit—Teachers are the reservoirs of this new spirit, the new spirit of adventure in intellectual matters, in social matters, in political matters. If you do not have that spirit, you cannot communicate that spirit to the youth, who are entrusted to your care.

Teacher must know what this country stands for and they must be able to communicate the vitality not merely the instruction.

Teacher to Set Example—It is education, it is instruction, it is knowledge and it is also the example which the teacher gives (Aggarwal 2002, pp. 260–61).[4]

Many of these paragraphs are self-explanatory. Not only did Radhakrishnan teach, but also always "walked the talk." I am tempted to reassert a few lines from the previous excerpts, only to display those innate qualities that the teacher needed to possess for building perceptiveness leading to performance, as indicated in the earlier parts of this Chapter. (Pages 17 and 18) ...*while giving tutorials to students at his residence, he used to receive students himself, offer tea and used to see them off at the door*...a clear instance of his empathy which he needed to demonstrate for building his rapport with students. ...*According to him a teacher should have openness of mind... The true teachers help us to think for ourselves in the new situations which arise*...an obvious indication of working as a mentor to evolve the student on his/her independent merits. ...*A good teacher must know how to arouse the interest of the pupil in the field of study for which he is responsible. He must himself be a master in the field of study and be in touch with the latest developments in the subjects*...the audience has to be kept engaged and there has to be continuing benchmarks created for upgrading oneself. ... *Only a teacher can give it (values) with his concrete quality. He that has (that concrete quality) must be a proper teacher who embodies truth and tradition, only those who have the flame in them can stir the five in others*...the highlight here is the role of passionate communication and the passing on of the values to the audience. ...*Teachers are the reservoirs of this new spirit, the new spirit of adventure in intellectual matters, in social matters, in political matters. If you do not have that spirit, you cannot communicate that spirit to the youth, who are entrusted to your care*...this is, I feel, a reinforcement of what has been said about maintaining repositories, bandwidth and passion in the chapter. Figure 2 will help in putting fingers on them.

---

[4] Aggarwal, J.C. 2002. *Philosophical and Sociological Perspectives on Education.* Shipra Publications.

Since we are discussing teachers, I wish to bring in a marked distinction between "withitness," a term coined by John Kounin in 1970 and perceptiveness here. "Withitness" is the art of running a classroom while having eyes in the back of your head. Kounin's model focuses on preventive discipline—techniques and strategies designed to prevent the occurrence of discipline problems in the first place, whereas perceptiveness is more inclusive—social background, ambitions, conduct, behavioral attributes and futuristic trends. Kathleen T. Talvacchia, B.S., M.Ed., Ed.D., Associate Dean for Academic and Student Affairs, Graduate School of Arts and Science, New York University in her book "Minds and Discerning Hearts—A Spirituality of Multicultural Teaching" (Chalice Press 2003) refers to Perceptive Attentiveness needed by teachers, which is closer to what we are trying to understand here. She unambiguously declares in her book,

.... Perceptive teachers hold the ability to keenly discern and sensitively understand themselves and their learners in all of their possibilities and limitations. Perceptive teachers in diverse learning environments focus specially on an awareness of the culture and social context of the learners and themselves.... Perceptiveness and Attentiveness focus both on others and ourselves. It is impossible to perceive others and be attentive to them if we are unable to perceive and be attentive to ourselves...

Our conclusion therefore, would be that perceptiveness is the only integrated approach that can propel the performance of a teacher and dispel the gospel of holding on fast to the prescribed norms of pedagogy that no doubt help you to launch yourself in the profession but keep your observations hindered in exploring what to do next.

... And What About Auteurs?

Credible information about this community undoubtedly reveals that creativity is one of the primary elements that each one possesses. When we watch a splendid motion picture, which has an impressionable "wow" factor, we notice the ingenuity of the maker and what contributions have flowed in to build such a marvelous creation. We comment, "Oh .... was in his elements!" How many of us ever ponder over the "observations" the maker had made, before spilling them out and reconstructing them into what we have just seen? The "out-of-box" thinking is what we keep harping about. But on what facts is the "out-of-box" thinking created? The more the facts, the more reliable is your thinking. What is it that lets the individual collect more facts in the same limited permissible time? Perceptiveness?

One of the first modern motion picture producers we can recall is Cecil B. DeMille the maker of "The 10 Commandments," which had surpassed all the pictures made thus far (1956) in its plot, the art and the technology used. Although the plot of the film was based on the Old Testament with the story of Moses as the highlight, DeMille researched beyond the Bible to collect facts. He tried and tested every actor in the lead roles right from Charlton Heston, Yul Bryner, Anne Baxter to the less significant ones. He went into the detailing of art, special effects and even the wardrobe, before taking a final call. It is said that in this movie, when Yvonne De Carlo, who was cast as Moses's wife Sephora, insisted that the western looks in her eyes need not be camouflaged with a contact lens, as she possessed grey eyes and that positioned her differently, he agreed much in misalignment with his firmness with other actors on this issue. That is the kind of detailing he went into. Why would not "The 10 Commandments" have been the most successful films of 1956 and the most financially successful film of that decade?

Cecil was born of Henry Churchill DeMille and Matilda Beatrice DeMille in 1881 in North Carolina, U.S.A. and inherited his passion for theatrics and biblical allegories from his father Henry, whereas the intelligence, the ardent desire to research and his strong will from Beatrice. The assortment of these attributes made Cecil become what he has been famous for. Cecil lost his father to a strange typhoid when he was just 12. It was the determination of his mother that took him and the family through all the turmoil, as his father had left no wealth. Cecil graduated from the American Academy of Dramatic Arts, where his father Henry was a faculty member at one point in time. He completed his studies on scholarship. Although Cecil started his career as an actor in the Broadway theatres also helping his brother who pursued his career as a playwright and also picking up assignments of producing plays, he couldn't achieve much success there. He had a wife and a baby daughter to support. He joined hands with Jesse Lasky, Samuel Goldwyn and some other East Coast business persons to launch Jesse L. Lasky Feature Play Company. Under this banner he labored hard with his crew, moving from place to place to shoot his first feature film "The Squaw Man," which was released in 1914. Cecil broke all conventions of making a 20 min film by making this film one hour long. He did not also follow the practice of shooting films at Edendale (where most studios were situated), but did so at Hollywood. The film created a sensation and not only did it establish the Jesse L. Lasky Feature Play Company, but also there was no looking back. After five years and 30 hit films, DeMille became Hollywood's most successful director. [Although the Lasky feature Play company had a shaky start, the company's success became assured when it joined with Adolph Zukor's Famous Players Films Company and Frank Garbutt's Bosworth, Inc. to distribute films through the newly formed Paramount Pictures Corporation headed by W. W. Hodkinson. In 1916 the three production companies merged to form the Famous Players-Lasky Corporation, and then assumed control of Paramount.]

The Roaring 20's were the boom years and DeMille took full advantage, opening the Mercury Aviation Company, one of America's first commercial airlines. He was also a real estate speculator, an underwriter of political campaigns, and a Bank of America executive, approving loans for other filmmakers.

Cecil B. DeMille

The arrival of the "talkies" did not deter the resolve that Cecil had. His resilience assisted him to transition his approach. He even devised a microphone boom, a soundproof camera blimp [housing] and also popularized the camera crane.

The Great Depression of the early 1930s took the toll on DeMille too. His M-G-M contract was not renewed, where he started his career with the "talkies." After years of success in Hollywood, DeMille, took a beating in the stock market collapse in 1929 and faced the challenge of being unemployed and nearly broke. However, Cecil managed to obtain a one-picture deal to produce and direct "The Sign Of The Cross." His old studio, Paramount, put up half the budget and DeMille financed the balance on his own. "The Sign Of The Cross" proved to be a tremendous hit, and DeMille remained with Paramount for the rest of his career. In 1936, he signed on as host of the Lux Radio Theater a dramatic anthology series that aired over the CBS radio network, and these radio appearances made Cecil B. DeMille a household name.

The following years saw many a stand of Cecil B. DeMille vis-à-vis the American Federation of Radio Artists and the Screen Directors' Guild as controversial and shrouded in mystery, but the conclusion one draws was that he was firm on what he stood for. Continuing with his filming and film-making Cecil put in his last straw for "The 10 Commandments," so much so that despite his having taken ill he finished the film with his shots in Egypt. Cecil died in 1959.

Here was a character who waged wars against all challenges, defied unprincipled actions and braved it up to prove that he was one of the greatest film-makers, the world had ever produced. There was no doubt that he stood by his passion, but how could he every time foresee his pursuit shadowed by danger and awaken his own self to greener pastures where his success lay? Indeed a fabulous insightfulness or a sense of perceptiveness that a man could capture and imbibe for all times to come. He kept himself informed and was alert to what was happening around him. So keen was he about his perfection to the tee that he and his perceptiveness worked round the clock till he breathed his last. Buried beneath a windswept sand dune, just outside the small farming town of Guadalupe on the central California coast, there lies a vast, century-old slab of Hollywood history. To realize his vision in the days before special effects, DeMille led a cast and crew of 3,500 to the desolate Guadalupe dunes, 150 miles north of Los Angeles, where carpenters crafted an ersatz Ancient Egypt from 168,000 meters of lumber, 11,000 kg of nails and 300 tons of plaster. The set was designed by Paul Iribe, one of the founders of the French Art Deco movement, who called for four 40-ton statues of Rameses the Great, eight imposing plaster lions, more than a dozen sphinxes and a 120ft-high backdrop of symbols and hieroglyphs. Memphis was rebuilt! This was in addition to his shots in Egypt.

Let us turn to another great film maker and this time from Asia—Akira Kurosawa—born on March 10, 1910, in Oimachi, a part of the Ōmori district of Tokyo, which was laced with a network of small rivers that were used by many locals in earlier times for drying harvested nori (a kind of a seaweed), a staple Japanese diet. It is worth mentioning here that the *Meiji* Restoration period in Japan spanned from 1868 to 1912, which had just ended when Akira was born, was actually responsible for the emergence of Japan as a modernized nation in the early 20th century. Father Isamu Kurosawa, a descendant of a samurai family from the northern Japanese island of Honshu and a Director of an Army physical education school, was therefore open to western traditions and considered theatre and motion pictures to have educational merit. He encouraged his children to watch films. As a consequence Akira was not only the captain of the school Kendo (a derivative of the Kenjitsu form of swordsmanship) team, but also went to see films as early as at the age of six.

Kurosawa was highly influenced by two other people in his early life—one was his primary school teacher, Seiji Tachikawa. "The fact that at such a time I encountered such free and innovative education with such creative impulse behind it....that I encountered a teacher like Mr. Tachikawa....I cherish among the rarest blessings," recounts Kurosawa in the book "The Warrior's Camera," by Stephen Prince. He inspired him to kindle his first passion and that was drawing and painting. Like all Japanese I have known personally, explaining complications through drawings or through pictures comes naturally; Kurosawa was no exception and was one who stood out exceptionally, because he had it in him as a trained talent. Later he used the technique to explain his themes to his crew in film-making as movie-frames.

The Kurosawa family was not poor. They had a servant in their household and might have been considered wealthy if not for Isamu's many dependents. Akira, the youngest sibling, had three older brothers (one of whom died before he was born) and four older sisters, Shigeyo, Haruyo, Taneyo, and Momoyo. At the time of Akira's birth, his oldest brother and sister were already adults, living outside the home and had started families of their own; Kurosawa spent his youth with the three younger sisters and his older brother Heigo, who was born in 1906. Heigo, was addicted to the novels of Fyodor Dostoyevsky and Maksim Gorky. He also introduced Akira to Western art and the auteur cinema of Fritz Lang, John Ford, Vsevolod Pudovkin, and Sergei Eisenstein. One specific incident which Kurosawa recollects is the aftermath of the Great Kantō earthquake that devastated Tokyo in 1923. Heigo took the 13-year-old Akira to view the destruction, and when the younger brother wanted to look away from the human corpses and animal carcasses which were scattered everywhere, Heigo stopped him and instead encouraged him to face his fears by confronting them directly. Although Heigo committed suicide when Akira was just 23 years old, he was the one who prepared him to face reality and empathize with the common man.

In the Kuroda Primary School, where Kurosawa went to, after his father's retirement and where he met his extraordinary teacher, Seiji Tachikawa, he also befriended Keinosuke Uekusa, who became a playwright and screenplay writer later and worked in collaboration with Akira.

Peggy Chiao the famous Taiwanese film critic writes,

The themes, symbolism, and aesthetic forms of Akira Kurosawa's films owe their origins to the ideas and sensibilities that captured his imagination as a young man. These include Marxism, which caught the attention of the Japanese intelligentsia in the 20's and 30's; classical Russian novels, which mesmerized the country's cultural elite; impressionist painting, which rocked the contemporary art world; and the sport of kendo, which Kurosawa practiced as a young boy.

Throughout the 1920s and early 1930s, Kurosawa pursued his love of literature and painting, and he wrote essays that were published in his class magazine. He became a leading student in these fields, while failing in subjects such as mathematics and compulsory military training, though the economic growth Japan had enjoyed in the 1910s gave way to runaway inflation and industrial unrest in the 1920s. The Great Kanto Earthquake was preceded by nationwide rice riots. Takashi Hara, leader of the "Taisho Democracy," was assassinated, and as older Meiji-era statesmen died off, the country became conservative and militaristic. Kurosawa's father, though a military man and an antisocialist, was appalled by the changes that were taking place. He was horrified by the 1923 murder of anarchist Sakae Osugi by militant extremists and the 1928 assassination of Manchurian warlord Chang Tso-lin by Japanese Army officers, along with the subsequent arrest of Japanese Communist Party members. Kurosawa might well have been pressed into military service himself if not for the sympathetic Army physician who remembered and respected his father. Upon his conscription examination in 1930, Kurosawa received the Japanese equivalent of 4-F status. Deemed physically unfit, he was never drafted, even in the last, desperate days of the Pacific War, when young boys and old men were pulled into active duty. "I often wonder what would have happened if I had actually been drafted," Kurosawa reflected in his autobiography.

But as Japan slid down further into economic depression, his family's finances grew bad to worse, and they moved again, this time to the Ebisu section of Shibuya, in Tokyo. Only gradually did it dawn on Kurosawa that each time his family moved, it was invariably to a smaller house, reflecting the worsening of their fortunes. In the late 1920s, oblivious to their situation, Kurosawa had decided that he wanted to become a painter. His father did not discourage him, but insisted he apply to art school. Kurosawa resisted such formal training, though, and failed to pass the entrance examination for the one art school to which he applied. Four months after Heigo's suicide, his oldest brother, Masayasu, died too, leaving Kurosawa his family's only surviving son. His ambitions to become an artist had gone almost nowhere, and he began to have doubts about his abilities. The economy and his personal finances were so bad he could not even afford paints and canvases. Japan had invaded China, and political turmoil was brewing all over the world.

Kurosawa spent the next two years aimlessly trying to see his future. Then, one day in late 1935, he saw an ad in a newspaper that changed the direction of his life. Photo Chemical Laboratories (or, as it was known, P. C. L.), a new film studio, was hiring assistant directors. Photo Chemical Laboratories was one of Japan's earliest film companies. It was bought in 1936 by Ichizo Kobayashi to form the production base that would become Toho. In 1941 and 1942, Kurosawa launched his writing career. The very next year, in 1943, he directed his first movie: *Sanshiro Sugata.* Five years later, Kurosawa met Toshiro Mifune and cast him in his 1948 movie *Drunken Angel.* Kurosawa cast Mifune many more times up until 1965, when after *Red Beard* the pair had a dispute and split their separate ways. His films have won many awards over the years, including academy awards, as he opened the world of Japanese cinema up to many movie-goers of the west. Many of his western admires have worked with him on projects, such as George Lucas, Francis Ford Coppola, Martin Scorsese and Steven Spielberg. Unfortunately, in Japan his films were not as highly regarded, and for the most part the Japanese public looked down on his obviously western influenced films. Thankfully, Kurosawa continued his work and became good friends with director Ishiro Honda, for who he collaborated with on most of his productions near the end of his career. Kurosawa crafted an utterly unique style that combines elements of traditional Japanese theatre (*Noh* drama and *kabuki,* for example) with an unparalleled sensitivity to the global reach of human dramas. His seemingly fearless willingness to tackle any theme, genre, or setting distinguished him as one of the most inventive directors of the 20th century. "The films of Akira Kurosawa join a deep sense of tradition with a commitment to artistic innovation—a combination that characterizes much of the best filmmaking in the Far East during the past 20 years," said Mark Winokur and Bruce Holsinger in year 2000.

Rashomon marked the entrance of Japanese film onto the world stage; it won several awards, including the Golden Lion at the Venice Film Festival in 1951, and an Academy Honorary Award at the 24th Academy Awards in 1952, and is now considered one of the greatest films ever made. We observe in most his pictures, as in Rashomon that repetition was essentially a component of Kurosawa, but the art of doing so creatively was not any man's cup of tea. Recurrence of the same act or similar acts in different perspectives and contexts would add colors to the situation and not appear to be repetitive but on the contrary be reiterative; and this can be seen through only by a perceptive person who has a wealth of capturing different situations and registering them. Another feature was "pauses" which helped the viewer to reflect and muse over his impressions. Now, here was a perceptive person keeping in mind the variance in the audience of comprehending the content in its appropriate context and also this was tantamount to giving his viewers time to grasp. The leaning on the west was displayed in many of his themes and that too emerged to assume another prominent character. How could a civilization that was distant and in the far-east yield a film maker with a grasp on such ideas? Childhood motivation from father Isamu to watch films from the west and appreciation for occidental events and readings that brother Heigo was pursuant of, left an indelible mark on Akira's thinking trends to evolve on his contemporariness and therefore his creations. The modern west could not be ignored by him, despite his emergence from a far-east culture. The world was already moving toward a global awareness and Akira Kurosawa was one of those early respondents who chose to respond positively. Of course, not a single film of his was bereft of humanism. The central characteristics highlighted here can nowhere else be born but in a film maker's perceptiveness. The credentials bestowed on Akira Kurosawa to receive the Ramon Magsaysay Memorial Award in 1965 (for the first time in eight years for a film personality) states "the Board recognizes his *perceptive* use of the film to probe the moral dilemma of man amidst the tumultuous remaking of his values and environment of the mid-20th century".... humanism was at the forefront for Akira.

In the late 1960s, the Japanese film industry was beginning to take a dip. Television was becoming popular. Looking at the international stature of Kurosawa, his dire need for work and his attempt to suicide in 1971, the then Soviet Union in 1973 invited him to direct Dersu Uzala, based on a Russian story which Kurosawa was attracted to since his assistant director days. This film again was awarded an Academy Award in 1976. I wish to recall the attention of readers to the life of Ernest Hemingway, who also could not take the downside befallen on him. Perceptiveness needs to be complemented with faith and resilience. The continued failure of acceptance of Kurosawa and his scripts in the commercial Japanese film world was because of high production costs and it was only because of his American admirers such as Francis Ford Coppola and George Lucas that 20th Century Fox agreed to purchase the international distribution rights of his film *Kagemusha*, which won the Cannes International Film Festival Golden Palm in 1980. Kurosawa died in 1998, after an arrest of his heart.

I cannot but let myself go not mentioning Satyajit Ray in this sequel. "The quiet but deep observation, understanding and love of the human race, which are characteristic of all his films, have impressed me greatly. ... I feel that he is a 'giant' of the movie industry," said Akira Kurosawa in 1975 about Ray.

Born on May 2, 1921 in Kolkata, in an affluent Bengali family which boasted of a rich heritage in art and literature, Satyajit Ray was the only son of Sukumar and Suprabha Ray. Upendrakishore Ray Chowdhury, also known as Upendrakishore Ray, who was a famous Bengali writer himself apart from being a painter, violin player and composer, technologist and entrepreneur, was Satyajit's grandfather. Kalinath Ray, the great grandfather was a scholar in Sanskrit, Arabic and Persian. He was expert in English and Persian languages and in the traditional Indian and British Indian legal systems. He became a topmost expert for interpreting old land deeds written in Persian and in helping the landowners to get the best deal from the newly introduced British legal system in India. He became affluent and in due course the family was able to afford two elephants. He belonged to Mymensingh—now Bangladesh. However, Upendrakishore was adopted by Harikishore—stated to be more old fashioned and a zamindar (feudal landlord) in the same area—a childless cousin of Kalinath.

This did not prevent Upendrakishore from shooting into prominence with his compositions for resurrecting the Brahmo Samaj—the small spiritually activist sect founded amongst the intelligentsia in Bengal by Raja Ram Mohan Ray to resist conversions into Christianity. Although, known for various hallmark contributions, his invaluable and unforgettable gift for the society was to establish and publish the magazine Sandesh for children, which has remained popular till today. Upendrokishore did not live long and was survived by his son, Sukumar who carried forward the legacy. He too was a trained printing technologist but preferred to write for children on nonconventional themes and in unconventional styles. His toil resulted in nonsensical masterpieces such as the assortment of poems *Abol Tabol* (Gibberish), the fable *HaJaBaRaLa* (The Absurdity), the collection of short stories *Pagla Dashu* (Crazy Dashu) and the play *Chalachitta Chanchari*.

Satyajit Ray had no ordinary background!

Satyajit had to move to his maternal uncle's house at the age of three along with his mother, as they had to quit their own lavishly spaced house, following changing of hands of the family printing business. His mother supplemented the family earning by teaching needle work and Satyajit went to the Ballygunge Government School, when he was eight. He proved to be an average student but was keener to go through film magazines that he stumbled upon, some of which were the like of the "Picturegoer" and the "Photoplay," which made him familiar with Hollywood. Also he cared to listen to Western Classical on gramophone records. When he was short of 15, he qualified the matriculation examination (school final) and his mother was intense about his higher education. He went to the Presidency College, starting with a graduation course in Science (first two years) and completed his graduation with Economics in the final year. Evidently over the years Ray's quest was inclined more toward films and film making and also toward compositions such that of Bach, Beethoven and Mozart rather than his allotted pursuit of academics. Eminent film-makers, such as Ernst Lubitsch, John Ford, Frank Capra, and William Wyler, caught his fancy and he became a loyal subscriber to Sight & Sound, a British monthly film magazine published by the British Film Institute.

Satyajit decided to give up further academic chase after his graduation in 1939 when he was 18. He sought an apprenticeship in commercial art, without having acquired any formal training. His mother insisted on such training, as she felt he was too young to be employed anywhere; and eventually he went to learn painting at Shantiniketan, after several reluctances…though not commercial art! It was difficult to ward away his mother's insistence and the lure of the proximity that Kavi Guru enjoyed with his father and grandfather. Young urban Satyajit got introduced to rural India through his outbound sketching excursions. Binode Behari Mukherjee, the art teacher was responsible for initiating Satyajit into homegrown and oriental art, including that from the Far East. He had been till then exposed only to the western forms. The interest in film making had germinated while in Shantiniketan amidst listening to Western Classical Music gramophone records and reading books on film making found in the library. The idea to make films however came in later. Rabindranath Tagore died in 1941 and Ray was back home in 1942. His intermittent visits to Kolkata were insufficient to quench his desire for being updated with the latest happenings, his love for his cousin Bijoya and above all the films that he missed including "Citizen Kane," a film by Orson Welles which had won many rave reviews.

By April 1943, Satyajit Ray had joined a British advertising agency, D.J. Keymer. He was taken in as a junior visualizer (kind of an apprenticeship). However, he spent 13 years here itself, learning the creative skills needed in the field. Ray was fascinated by typography—remember the art of printing ran in the blood—both that of Bengali and of English and created numerous ground-breaking advertising campaigns. ("Ray Roman" and "Ray Bizarre," which were his designed type-faces [fonts], won an international competition in 1971). He brought in more of Indian motifs and calligraphic elements to advertising. This love for typography and illustration would often surface in the credits and the publicity posters of his films, later. His senior colleague at D. J. Keymer, D. K. Gupta started a publishing house "Signet Press"* and Ray was roped in to do the cover jackets. In 1944, D. K. Gupta decided to bring out an abridged version of a novel by Bibhuti Bhushan Banerjee, Pather Panchali. Until then, Ray had not read much of Bengali literature. By his own admission, he was still unfamiliar with many of Tagore's works. Ray was asked to illustrate the abridged version of the novel. The book itself made a lasting impression. D. K. Gupta, also a former editor of a Bengali film magazine, told Ray that the abridged version of the book could make a very good film.

This long association with D. K. Gupta's Signet Press for designing covers and illustrations for books granted Satyajit Ray with an opportunity to read Bengali literature. Some of the books, he designed the jackets for, were later adapted by him for his films.

The World War II having got over, there was a spillage of American cinema in Kolkata and Satyajit made his best to watch as many. In 1947, with a few friends such as Bansi Chandra Gupta, Ray cofounded Calcutta's first film society which screened Battleship Potemkin as the first. With his flair for writing Ray started contributing to film magazines and newspapers both in English and Bengali. Writing screenplays was another passion that he developed soon. One of his friends, Harisadhan Dasgupta had acquired rights for producing Tagore's "Ghare Baire" and Ray wrote the screenplay. The film was never produced as Ray would not budge from changing his script, as insisted by a doctor friend of the producer. Ghare Baire was produced 35 years later with Ray finding his earlier attempt an amateurish one.

In 1949, Jean Renoir had come to Kolkata to shoot his film "The River." Satyajit made it a point to see him in the hotel that he was staying in; and soon impressed with the knowledge of films that he possessed, Renoir saw to it that he was travelling with him in the drive to identify locations. He even shared with him his outline and the illustrations that he had made for Pather Panchali, when Renoir asked him if he was planning to make a film. Although Ray wanted to be a part of *Incidentally Signet Press had also published two books of Satyajit Ray's father Sukumar Ray; Abol-Tabol (meaning Hocus-Pocus) and Ha-ja-ba-ra-la (meaning Higgledy Pigleddy).

This film making unit, he couldn't, because he was transferred to its London office by D. J. Keymer, where he had already become the Art Director. Before departing for London, Satyajit had married his cousin Bijoya who was deeply interested in his films and music.

A business trip to London in 1950 proved a turning point. Ray and wife travelled to London by ship, a journey that took 16 days. With him, he was carrying a notebook in which he had made some notes on making a film of Pather Panchali. In this six-months long stay abroad, Ray must have seen about a hundred films including Vittorio De Sica's "Bicycle Thieves." "Bicycle Thieves" made a profound impression on Ray. Later, in the introduction of "Our Films, Their Films," (a collection of articles written by him between 1948 and 1971) he wrote- "All through my stay in London, the lessons of Bicycle Thieves and neo-realist cinema stayed with me." The film had reconfirmed his conviction that it was possible to make realistic cinema with an almost entirely amateur cast and shooting at actual locations.

Upon his return Satyajit lost no time in putting things together. In the perspective of not having any film-making experience, he gathered young men with different backgrounds as technicians, such as Subrata Mitra, who was actually a still photographer but was literally cajoled into the role of a cinematographer. In order to make his ideas about the film more comprehensible to the potential producers, Satyajit carried a small note-book, filled with sketches, dialogue and the treatment. Producers were intrigued and overjoyed with this script along with another sketchbook that illustrated the key dramatic moments of the film, but while many of them were impressed, none came forward to produce the film. The editorial team of "Probashi," an e-magazine on Art and Culture comments thus,

A part time director, using his personal finances, with a cast of amateur actors and a crew who were first timers, pulled off a miracle. If perseverance is stubbornness with a purpose, making of Pather Panchali is an apt example.

Two years were lost in the search for a producer. The persistence, which was so intense, drove Rayto begin building on a belief that unless he had a few shots or a part of the film ready, he would not be able to successfully scout around for a legitimate producer. On borrowed money against his insurance policy and small loans from dear friends, Ray ventured with his team into unusual outdoor locations to make parts of the film. There were many dampening remarks from the conventional film makers who were dependent on studio shooting for natural happenings such as rain. Against all odds Ray captured the rain shots in the midst of Kans Grass

(Saccharum spontaneum) with his amateur cast, only to postpone his second shot to the following year, as stray cattle had grazed the fields captured in the first shot. While the efforts to push through the shots with a mix of mostly amateur artistes and a few professional screen or stage actors were on, untiring endeavors to spot a producer continued. Bimal Roy's "Do Bighaa Zameen" (Half an acre of land) made in 1952 had many natural outdoor shots and its winning the Prix International at *the Cannes festival in 1954 and Kurosawa's "Rashoman," emboldened Ray with* the trend he was following in film making. Ray discovered for himself,

> *how to catch the hushed stillness of dusk in a Bengali village when the wind drops and turns the ponds into sheets of glass, dappled by the leaves of Saluki and Shale, and the smoke from the ovens settles in wispy trails over the landscape and the plaintive blows on conch shells from homes far and near are joined by the chorus of crickets which rises as the light falls, until all one sees are the stars in the sky, and the stars that blink and swirl in the thickets.*

In 1953, the find for a producer ended with Ana Dutta, who promised more funds after watching the results following the release of his last film. Satyajit embarked on his shooting mission and even took leave for a month from D. J. Keymer to achieve what he wished (till now he was shooting only at weekends) to. But soon he discovered that the promise the producer had made could not be fulfilled, as his last film was a disaster. The project started running out of funds and Ray had to pledge Bijoya's jewelery as a collateral (the last alternative an Indian would opt for) to keep the work going, only for a few days more. Ray returned to his agency. The footage Ray had covered was edited, but there were no takers for funding the project further. Ray's Production Manager Anil Choudhury suggested that the then Chief Minister of West Bengal, Dr. B. C. Roy be approached, which worked and the Government agreed to fund the film. In this situation of turmoil, September 1953 also saw the birth of his son Sandeep. Ray resumed the work after one whole year in 1954. The money from the Government was being released in installments and replenishment of funds was happening only after accounts for previous expenses were submitted. Ray had to cope with it.

Monroe Wheeler, a director of Museum of Modern Art (MOMA) and its head of the department of exhibitions and publications, New York came to Kolkata in the autumn of 1954 to collect certain Indian highlights for an exhibition. Ray perchance bumped into him and laid down some stills from his films. Wheeler offered to hold a world premier at MOMA. Ray's work was validated by John Huston the maker of "The man would be King" who came to India six months later in search of locations. Having watched only a 15 to 20 min silent rough-cut, John Huston was convinced. His evaluation submitted to Wheeler, paved the way for the film to premier at MOMA. Once the deadline for the premier was set, it was day and night work for Ray. Satyajit had settled for Pandit Ravi Shankar the famous sitar maestro to score the music for the film, but the latter had very little time to spare as he was mostly travelling. Just as John Huston did, Ravi Shankar saw but only half of the film and composed the music in one go of 11 hours. Though exhausted, Ray was quite happy with the outcome. The film could be finalized only a night before the day of its dispatch. Weeks after the screening at MOMA, a letter arrived from them. It was strewn with accolades of how well it was accepted even without the subtitles! In 1955, just a few months later, Kolkata saw the release of the film with the audience gradually picking up numbers and eventually packed theatres. B.C. Roy the Chief Minister of West Bengal was so impressed that he wanted Jawaharlal Nehru, the then Prime Minister to watch the film in his ensuing visit to Kolkata. Nehru recommended the film as India's entry to the Cannes' Film Festival of 1956. It was a fight till the end. Since the screening was scheduled at midnight the jury was missing as France has a "holiday season" then (the Labour Day, the Ascension Day etc.) A special screening was organized with the full jury, despite this, and the film won "The Best Human Document" prize. Ray had done it!

From then onwards there was no looking back. Not only what followed were great compliments, tributes and awards both at home and abroad, but also Ray had decided to quit his job at D. J. Keymer and take a plunge into film making. Notwithstanding the fact that he had become a world class director, he had set a benchmark for Indian Cinema and his films that followed had to be better than the one before. He created the Apu Trilogy as a sequel to Pather Panchali, that being inclusive, Aparajito in 1956 and Apur Sansar 1959. Sunil Singh, of San Francisco Bay, who maintains and monitors the site SatyajitRay.org says,

Until 1981, he would make a feature length film every year. His later films included—Parash Pathar (The Philosopher's Stone 1958), Jalsaghar (The Music Room 1958), Devi (The Goddess 1960), Teen Kanya (Two Daughters 1961), Kanchenjungha, (1962), Charulata (The Lonely Wife 1964), Pratidwandi (The Adversary 1970), Shantranj Ke Khilari (The Chess Players 1977), and Ghare-Baire (Home and the World 1984).

On March 30, 1992, Ray was honored with a "lifetime achievement" award [Honorary Academy Award], while he was in the Hospital on his deathbed by the Academy of Motion Picture Arts and Sciences. Ray died on April 23, 1992 and did not live to see the India Ratna (the highest award of India) awarded to him the same year.

There can be none better a description of the essence of Ray's films than

... when Satyajit Ray did his films you suddenly not understood the culture because the culture was so complex but you became attached to the culture through the people, and it didn't matter what they were speaking, what they were wearing, what their customs were. Their customs were very, very interesting and surprising, and you suddenly began to realize there are other cultures in the world ...

Film Director Martin Scorsese thus paid his tributes to Satyajit Ray, in Washington Post, February 28, 2002.

The three great film makers that we have seen, came not only from different social backgrounds and cultural heritages, but also from dissimilar geographical surroundings, yet we found many attributes common. What stood out are their aspirations of putting in their best to every creation of theirs through untiring persistence. And what is remarkably astonishing is the rebel in them that loaded them to push unforeseen themes and techniques for filming. Incidentally, today, there is a throb in the management world to recognize rebel thoughts that are constructive, so as to enable effective employee engagement.

But what eventually gets displayed as a common feature in their personalities and also their works, is their contextual comprehension of the contemporary milieu, the timely mention of the issues, the need to introspect them and possible alternatives to redress them. Alertness to every single happening and the social awareness of behavioral indicators of different characters portrayed that had been registered by them for embedding in their theme for filming had been outstanding.

Notwithstanding the fact that all three film makers served their audiences a potion that had a blend of changing mores in society, essentially there's no second thought that their individual perceptiveness had played its inevitable role. While Cecil B. DeMille brought forth epical features in a style that was acceptable to the contemporary world, Kurosawa and Ray went into the critical detailed perspectives of their respective hinterland and its backdrop. Had it not been for the eye for detail and every tiny bit indexed in the mind for reproduction at the appropriate time, their performances would not have been what we witness today and what they have become famous for.

Some Validation of the Aforesaid Illustrations

The array of personalities highlighted thus far is, in fact substantial biographical evidence to demonstrate how, irrespective of their vocations, perceptiveness worked for stalwarts and which is why they did become stalwarts, whom history is proud to recount. However, this evidence is more like a ballad leading us to a belief rather than a structured correlation of facts which could usher in a conclusion. No work would be complete without an empirical study to indicate the correlation. Therefore this compilation would have been left unconvincing if one had opted out of an attempt to substantiate the postulates with contemporary data and their analyses.

An attempt to address a heterogeneous audience was a priority. The heterogeneity was spread amongst different vocations, age groups, nationalities and cultures, covering South Asia, South East Asia, the Middle East, Europe, and the United States. *Onehundred* participants were shortlisted based on these factors of heterogeneity and the trends were observed. Here's the simplistic questionnaire that was used—a set of 10 close ended questions.

The Questionnaire

1. *Can you see what's happening behind you, when surrounded by known people?*
2. *Do you overhear other conversations and pretend not to?*
3. *When you are preoccupied, how frequently do you sense that there are things happening around you?*
4. *When you sense things are happening around you, do you respond to all?*
5. *Do you think you can discern between unusual happenings from usual ones, when you are preoccupied?*

6. *What adds to your immediate understanding of a situation/person?*

7. *Do you make serious efforts to find out how your behavior has been viewed by the person with whom you have been interacting?*

8. *Do you carefully observe how a person takes what you tell him/her, and then accordingly communicate?*

9. *Do you tend to categorize people and situations in terms of your previous assessments of similar nature and frame them thus?*

10. *Which of the following personality attributes describes you best?*

The intention of keeping the number of questions to only 10 was to go with the expectation that time was the biggest scarcity in all professions irrespective of culture or location. Secondly, people were averse to answering too many questions, even if they were closed ended, unless someone was habitually keen to answer inventory based probes. Also the small number of closed ended questions were discreetly picked and worded so that correlations could be deduced easily without having to connect too many of them to construct the chain leading to the findings. Each question has been explained with its objective and the answers depicted graphically in order to elucidate the causative analysis. The deductions drawn so far in this work in the form of statement of historical facts and description of personalities are well validated through this research. Every question and its replies have only reiterated them.

The first question: *Can you see what's happening behind you, when surrounded by known people?*

The explanation: Here the respondent has to understand the context in which the question has been asked. "See" does not literally convey that the respondent is physically able to see with the use of his/her eyes. But instead, it is to query, if one is able to visualize the broad sequence of events or conversation taking place, when one is not around amongst people who are well acquainted with the respondent.

The answers: Four options were provided and the replies have been tabulated as follows.

Answers	Percentage
Yes, very clearly	19.59
No, not at all	13.4
To some extent	65.98
Others	1.03

The graphical representation of the responses:

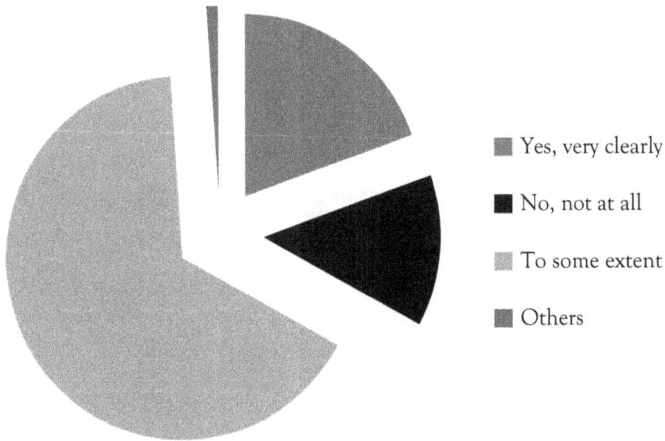

- Yes, very clearly
- No, not at all
- To some extent
- Others

This is a direct question to ascertain perceptiveness going by the definition enumerated in the earlier part of the book, (titled as *Introduction*). Based on one's observations of a person's behavioral responses to situations and behavior one has to use his/her alertness to comprehend the pattern. Once that is done one begins to have premonitions in the direction that would coincide with facts. Every person would possess this attribute but the variation would be that of the degree of accuracy. Two factors contribute to accuracy—correctness of observations and the intensity of alertness.

Amongst our respondents there were 13.4 percent, who honestly admitted that they were not able to "see" and another 1.03 percent who avoided answering directly or chose to reply in a vague manner for they did not have a positive answer or possibly didn't perceive the question and its context. It does not mean that they (13.4 percent plus 1.03 percent) were not keen observers or they weren't alert enough. It only meant that both their social awareness and alertness didn't work for them simultaneously. Since we are looking at a continuum, those stating that they could "see" to some extent only were subjected to distractions while making sequential observations, dissuading the consistency needed. Let us concede that inconsistency in alertness brings about inconsistency in observations and therefore adds to the inaccuracies in registering them in the repositories of our memories. A large majority that is, 65.98 percent fell in this category. Not that the entire 19.59 percent were to be accepted as those who could comprehend well, but it is such percentages are always small and the fact regarding their "sensibilities" are corroborated through other questions here. The term "social awareness," has been used throughout this book, liberally. It refers to *the presence of signals that are aroused from the senses of sight, smell, touch, taste or hearing and that may relate to human personalities, to situations or even to inanimate or animate objects (experienced)*" part of the definition. Daniel Goleman the founding thinker on Emotional Intelligence describes social awareness as the tool that shows how people handle relationships through awareness of others' feelings, needs, and concerns. Matthew Lieberman the neuro-social scientist from University of California refers to it as the "the mind wandering circuitry that directs us to think about other people's minds—their thoughts, feelings, and goals" in his book *Social: Why Our Brains Are Wired to Connect.*[5]

The Second Question: *Do you overhear others' conversations and pretend not to?*

The explanation: Constrained by ethical norms we attempt to rein in our senses and desist from overhearing anyone else's conversation. Human beings as we are, however, we do overhear. It is another thing that such communication just pours into our ears and we do not register the words. Or our mind unconsciously chooses some words (more or less) to register, while in some instances every word registers even if there is no deliberate move to do so and there are other instances when you make those deliberate attempts, dropping the ethics aside. Therefore the

---

[5] Social: Why Our Brains Are Wired to Connect by Matthew D. Lieberman published by Oxford University Press.

instinct varies from not registering to embedding every word or at least the logical construct derived from such words. The hypothesis is that the more perceptive you are the greater would be your inventory enabled to record and remember.

The answers: Again four options were provided and the replies have been tabulated as follows.

Answers	Percentage
Yes, mostly	19.19
Yes sometimes, if I am doing something, where a lot of concentration is not needed	59.6
No, never	18.18
Others	3.03

The graphical representation of the responses:

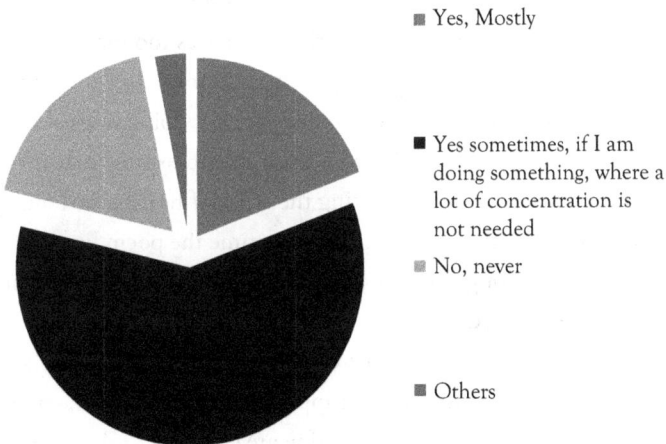

- Yes, Mostly
- Yes sometimes, if I am doing something, where a lot of concentration is not needed
- No, never
- Others

The respondents who have stated "no, never" are either scared of exposing themselves to a highly ethical society or the ethics prohibiting someone to overhear are very deeply ingrained (18.18 percent). Those responding with variable responses in the "others" category, have not led to any logical conclusions (3.03 percent). Hence shall be clubbed with the earlier "negative" responses. A bulk of the responses (59.6 percent) has said "sometimes." Honest answers with the fear of losing control over their objective of what they were trying to achieve. Attention has got divided, which is only natural, while pursuing a task. Only a few said that they mostly overheard such conversations (19.19 percent).

Once I was training a bunch of executives in an open house program on "listening skills"...I dubbed a beautiful poem on the subject of listening with a background of *Gaur Saarang*, an Indian Raga [literally...a melody...or one of the melodic modes used in traditional...Indian classical music] by the famous Pt. Bhimsen Joshi and asked the participants to read the poem well. After the display of the lines of the poem, done slower than acceptable norms, participants had to confess as to what they were doing, whether listening to the music or reading. Some said they were doing both. Probed further on the content of the poem or about the music, this lot failed to respond satisfactorily. There was another group which said that the music came in their way of concentrating on the lines and compelled them to take more time than usual to comprehend the lines. However, they made their answers explicable, with a greater zest than what had been observed in the last group. Then there was this another group which confessed that the music was too mesmerizing and they caved in to that and eventually gave up on comprehending the poem, without the fear of being held accountable for not doing the task assigned on time. This was the bolder lot who were able to express that they were not prepared to sacrifice experiencing the sense of hearing (listening), for they were confident that given a little more time the poem lines would be well understood through already mastered skills of reading and cognition, if the music was muted.

The responses to the previous question have been on similar lines. While it is vital to do a task with full application of one's mind, senses such as seeing, hearing, smelling and touching are ever alert and are wandering as Liebermann the social neuroscientist states. More than 2,500 years ago Buddha was teaching people about the human mind with a different purpose, so that they might understand themselves better and discover that there was a way out of suffering. Buddha too described the human mind as drunken monkeys, jumping around, screeching, chattering and carrying on endlessly. We all have monkey minds, Buddha said, with dozens of monkeys all clamoring for attention, in response to stimuli—external and internal. Reading and writing on the other hand emerge as an outcome of skills. However rapt an attention one may possess to express the skills, it does not overrule the senses. This is what determines the degree of perceptiveness even if it is at the cost of efficiency to perform the task assigned, definitely not at the cost of productivity though. Another dimension which we may not ignore is that even among the senses, the use of sight and touch is a voluntary activity while hearing and smelling are not and continue to be involuntary, unless you walk out of the environment. Therefore it is not a matter of choice whether you want to hear or smell. They reach you even if you do not want to receive the signals. Therefore it is only the mind that filters and decides what to store and what to scrap.

One's alertness to communication, situations and the contexts is one essential contributory factor in one's perceptiveness. The other is of course the recognizing them and storing them for a recall whenever needed. Wherever the accountability factor is mightier than one's receptivity to surroundings, perceptiveness takes a dip. This fact would be discussed at greater length, when correlations are examined.

The Third Question: *When you are preoccupied, how frequently do you sense that there are things happening around you?*

The explanation: Principally this is a basic question which ought to have been asked in the beginning, but has been strategically placed as the third question in the sequence, so that the responses are easier to validate. Do you not find it similar to the First Question? If you can actually sense occurrences of routine nature without making an extra effort your alertness is undoubtedly sharp. Alertness is indisputably one of the contributory factors toward effective perceptiveness but such alertness all by itself is incapable of enhancing the latter. It inevitably needs to be complemented with a high nous of "social awareness," defined earlier.

The answers: The four options and their responses have been tabulated as follows.

Answers	Percentage
Always	23.23
Sometimes	64.65
Never	9.09
Others	3.03

The graphical representation of the responses:

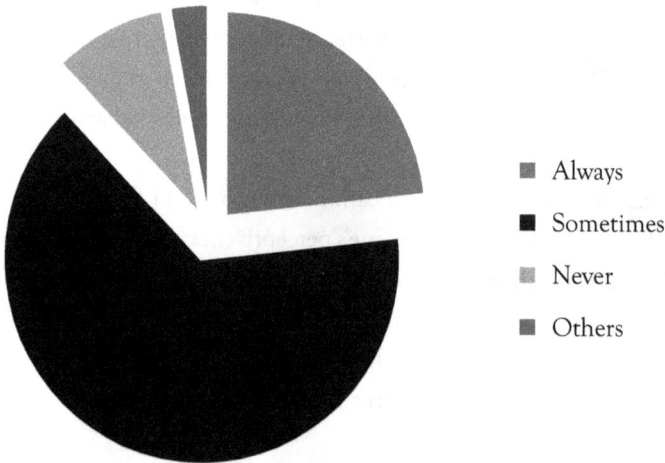

- Always
- Sometimes
- Never
- Others

23.23 percent have boldly stated that they always do. This only means that they were more alert than the rest. It does not let us conclude that this was a measure of perceptiveness. However, this attribute is invariably an essential component of perceptiveness, and is complemented by social awareness as already stated in the explanation. 64.65 percent state that they sometimes do, which meant that their alertness to such things happening was wavering and which is quite natural. 9.09 percent have refused to recognize noticing such things happen and 3.03 percent have left us with unconcerned answers. I remember the story that our Chemistry teacher in IX standard had told us. "In a classroom a teacher was talking about the role of a catalyst to the students, when in order to check back he asked a student if the latter could repeat what the former had explained. The student replied, "Sir, the lizard on the wall has gone into the hole next to the skylight!" Are you fellows listening? Do you see how attentive this student was?" Now, let us see the relevance of the story.

The student talking about the lizard was oblivious to what was happening in the classroom because his interest lay in the wall lizard making its moves, rather than the story about the catalyst. His alertness to what was happening around him was absolutely focused on the lizard and he did *not* know about anything else occurring. The 9.09 percent are like this student absolutely focused on to their preoccupation. 64.65 percent are of the kind who perhaps were also watching the lizard but whose attention kept oscillating between "the role of the catalyst" and the movement of the lizard, only sometimes, depending on their interest levels. Guessing it right perhaps the percentage of those watching the lizard would be much less, as the lizard was noiseless. We have seen that we succumb to involuntary senses more than the voluntary ones and also the interest levels perhaps were diminished…"Catalyst" was new. They had all seen wall lizards before! Therefore what you wish to see, touch, hear and smell depends on your interest level in the subject too. Involuntary senses receive the signals you are not interested in, but do not register or even get to reject them! What this goes to determine, is illustrated in the following equation.

Alertness ∞ Interest

Now this ferries us into asking ourselves the next query as to, how does one build on quicker social awareness if focus comes in one's way, when social awareness is the other key to perceptiveness. If alertness is so dependent on interest, one would be confined within limitations to record data pertaining to one's interest only. (Does that mean that a perceptive person has multifarious interests? We shall come back to this soon, as at this stage it is more significant to document the findings of the research conducted with our sample audience.)

Our next question (the fourth question) is intertwined with the question asked here (the third question) and goes to verify one's ability to at least make an effort to address the issues small or big highlighted through the alertness displayed.

The Fourth Question: *When you sense things are happening around you, do you respond to all?*

The explanation: Let us understand that the response to things around you would be elicited, only if you sense them. But sometimes you sense them and yet do not respond. Is it a choice that you exercise? And going a step further is it a choice based on your interest level or is it a social compulsion? If we assume for a while that it is the latter, it is certain that you are doing so because you value the relationship/s ... you are a people's person ... you are curious about the person or the situation/s in which the people were. Is that curiosity for your own understanding and comprehension for a recall later or is it for an immediate proactive response? In both cases your presence is noticed especially when you are amongst known people. If it is the former it could be just for quenching your thirst for figuring out what is what and record the experience for your own understanding.

The answers: Again four options were provided and their responses have been tabulated as follows.

Answers	Percentage
Yes, I try to manage all	18
Yes, only to unusual ones	68
Do not pay heed to them at all	12
Others	2

The graphical representation of the responses:

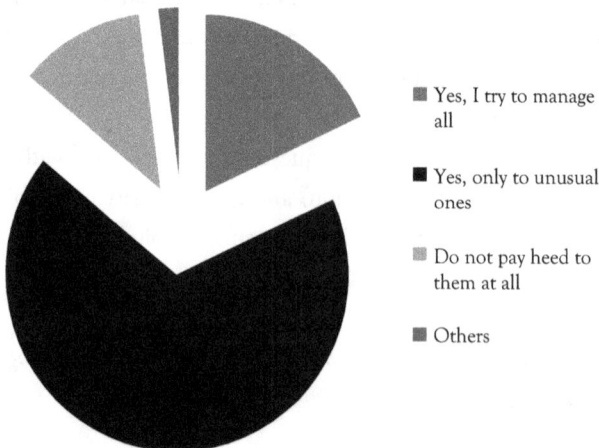

- Yes, I try to manage all
- Yes, only to unusual ones
- Do not pay heed to them at all
- Others

When 18 percent say that they try to manage all, they are surely expressing so with a certain confidence. Most of us are conscious that one of the vital sources of confidence is awareness—of how to manage. This means not only do these respondents know what was happening but also as to why it was happening, what would resolve the issue if it was a problem and what would help escalating it if it was a proactive contribution. This leads to the finding that such persons are socially aware of the intricacies of behavioral responses and what directions were to be provided. The only limitation to such persons is time and that is why the use of the word, "try." A large majority would be drawn to unusual happenings as they are riddled off the cuff and receive a jerk in their accepted process of thinking as to what would follow what. Here the approach normally would be to attend to the happenings when one is off what, one is involved in. The social awareness does prevail in them but not to that extent as in the case of those who were more confident. That is why that extra focused time is needed to comprehend, or in other words create that social awareness, when not involved in anything else. The unusual happenings catch their alertness just as a spelling mistake in a sentence would, or a discordant note in a piece of melody would or an obnoxious smell in a clean environment would or the touch of a hot metal would. Therefore the alertness also remains subdued unless something unusual happens. In the case of others this alertness is constrained because of their being overpowered by the needed focus, for which perhaps extra efforts were required.

The allusion to the great Mahabharata, where *Dronacharya* the Guru is full of appreciation on receiving a response from *Arjuna* saying, "I see nothing but the eye of the bird" will definitely not be worth it, in today's context. Such illustrations may be worthwhile only when concentration is explained, but surely not when perceptiveness is. The alertness to wider range of activities and situations is the call of the day. And the knowhow of how to control them would be derived from the practiced skill of wider social awareness. A very aptly put thought by the famous French novelist, Marcel Proust, "The voyage of discovery is not in seeking new landscapes but in having new eyes."

The Fifth Question: *Do you think you can discern between unusual happenings from usual ones, when you are preoccupied?*

The explanation: This is actually in continuation to the commentaries made in the answers to the previous question, rather a step beyond. The question is about focus or concentration. Are you Arjuna of the Mahabharata times or Arjuna required to be in the millennial generation, when the flow of information is incessant and that too from a variety of sources? Will you be focused on your immediate goal and let other information go by? Such information may not come to you again or it may, when you have already learnt it through someone else who has a "one-up" on you and you discover that it might have been vital in this competitive and innovative race for mere survival, let alone you proving to be outstanding. Can you afford not to discriminate between the unusual from the usual or do you need to go beyond, to comprehend the routine or usual as well, and comprehend the finer discernments? It may seem contradictory to what we have been indoctrinated with since childhood. Focus, concentration, no-distraction were beautiful words with the Arjuna's role model as an ideal. Not that they cease to be! But the concentration or focus now stands challenged with the much needed information or data that has a continuous inflow. Your focus is needed at multiple places. Are we not living in the era of multitasking and preparing to equip ourselves accordingly? There has been a paradigm shift. The question has been asked to find out if one is able to identify the basics or one is adept in going beyond the fundamentals.

The answers: The respondents are again of four categories—A. Those confident B. Those who are on the brink and need that extra effort C. The traditional "Arjunas" and D. Do not fathom the seriousness of the question.

Answers	Percentage
Yes of course	18
Make an effort to put all my senses into action	68
Can comprehend only when I am off what	
I was doing	12
Others	2

The graphical representation of the responses:

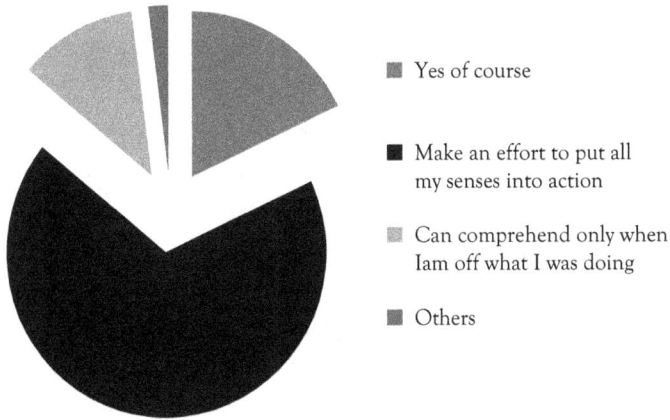

Of the surveyed respondents, those who felt that it was no uphill task at all to distinguish between the extraordinary from the ordinary, while being preoccupied with something else, were just about 18 percent. "Yes, of course" indicates the confidence and also gets to reveal the respondent's mindset to be in the frame, "What's the big deal? I thought you wanted me to find out something more!" These are the millennial Arjunas, who could sense things happening around them whether there was a striking note in the midst of the routine or not. We have had such millennial Arjunas from time immemorial and in this book we have cited exemplary sagas about personalities who are ensconced with this attribute that is so relevant in the 21st century. Sixty eight percent were found having to make that little extra effort to capture the awareness needed to comprehend the sequence of events and their causes. In this lot, would it not be safe to conclude that (1) they were the majority [the survey shows so], (2) they could sense things only with that extra effort, which did not come to them naturally and that (3) they were not oblivious (social awareness was awakened) but needed a push? They need to gear up, while 12 percent are the traditional Arjunas. These are the people who have to change their understanding. Their perspective of focus and concentration are outdated in the contemporary world. They have to work on the mindset change. The others that is, 2 percent are clueless about what they need to do.

The normal probability theory would apply to the process of distinguishing the unusual from the usual. In general, probability is a measure of the likelihood of some outcome. We use it not to describe what will happen in one particular event, but rather, what the long-term proportion that outcome will occur.

Let us recall Shahaji's numerous battles mentioned in "The Parley." He was conversant (socially aware) with how the Mughal and the Nizam armies would respond, especially when his own army was phenomenally outnumbered. He was also conversant with the terrain, the topography, the geography, the season in the year and the dynamics of a river dam. The solution therefore was not far away particularly when the ways of guerrilla warfare was also something he was accustomed to. Let us see the emphasis that he built on his thinking in numerous directions with the grasp of knowledge and awareness on a variety of subjects. The unusual that prompted him to think differently was the well equipped humungous numbers available to the foe. As a valiant soldier, he could have well fought the battle till total destruction, as many Rajput kings of this country had done. But approaching more recent times, as a strategist and as a leader his approach was different. He noticed the unusual very fast only to respond quickly from his inventory of awareness and devastated the enemy. His focus was tracking over different things simultaneously—from the camping site of the gigantic size of the opponent, to the river in full flow to the loosening of the civil work in the dam to the terrain of the land. The most spectacular aspect was that these were made to happen in quick succession or almost simultaneously—which was possible because of this tracking of a few multiple things, he was confidently aware of—in a spontaneous response. It can be argued that such strategies in warfare have been cited in the epics as well, such as that of the Trojan Horse in the Iliad or the Chakravyuh in the MahaIndiaa. But let us not overlook the fact that we were made to believe in reference to those stories from the epics. All those strategies were carried out with ample planning and time at one's disposal. Shahaji had to execute his strategy overnight before day break. It was only and only achievable because of the alertness (tracking ability) and social/general awareness that he possessed about the stretch and the region. He was a millennial Arjuna living in the medieval period!

The Sixth Question: *What adds to your immediate understanding of a situation/person?*

The explanation: Most of us judge people while interacting with them, unless it is a one-time query that you are making or replying to a passerby who is asking for directions to a place. Even in that short while we start asking ourselves as to why that question was asked, or what could be the reason for that person looking for that place, and so on. It is man's fundamental nature to be judgmental, whether rational or biased or illogically guided by one's fancies. This is the reason as to why we query ourselves to find an answer which could eventually lead us to the judgment. Let us examine what are usually the guidelines for a person to conclude on a perception/judgment/understanding. Alfred Otara from the Kigali Institute of Education, Rwanda spells them out in his article, "Perception: A Guide for Managers and Leaders" published in Vol. 2, No. 3; September 2011 of the Journal of Management and Strategy by Sciedu Press. They have been simplified as Habit, Motivation, Learning, Specialization and Social Background. How many times do we mistake a heavy vehicle passing by our house for an earthquake? Those who live in earthquake prone belts are often left bewildered, when they in due course find that it was only a heavy eight wheeler trailer making its way. This perception has arisen because of *habit.* If you are busy writing a project report in your study, when someone is watching a cricket match on the television in the living room and you hear the spectators raising a humdrum, what is your understanding? A four, a six or someone clean bowled, that is if you are interested in cricket. If you are not then it is cacophony. This is a simple illustration of interest and *motivation* leading to a perception. The demonetization drive of the Indian nation categorically highlighted the distinction between the learned and the not so learned. Here the learning refers to the ability to use Internet banking and move toward a cashless economy or the inability to do so for whatever reason. Those unable, find the whole movement as something that has jeopardized their only means of transacting. This is a characteristic example of how a perception could come to stay if one has not enough *learning,* about what one has to do. A death in the family will have the neighborhood policeman make enquiries if there was anything unusual. Your lawyer friend would query you if all papers regarding inheritance were in order. Then there is the recluse who would philosophize the situation and talk about the good and the bad "karma." If you have a physician in the family and was not present when the person died, he would probably probe into medical reasons of the death and give you bits on what could have been done as an alternative. This is how *specializations* influence perceptions. I have had relatives visiting me from my village on occasions of an initiation ceremony or a wedding or even a death for that matter. They are awe-struck when we consciously overrule certain rituals, which we felt were irrelevant in urban globalised living. Perhaps we are in for a criticism back in our village. Well that is not where we were socialized and there-fore it did not matter to us if they had strong objections because of their *social background.*

Perceptions guide every interaction. Therefore your understanding, however rational you may try to be, stands influenced by your percep-tions. You could only minimize such influence but not eliminate them. Among the factors that Otara has mentioned, learning plays a very sig-nificant role in minimizing the influence of your perception-constructs built as a result of other reasons listed by him. The more (facts) you know about a situation or a person, easier it becomes for your understanding irrespective of whether you are present or not.

Answers	Percentage
Experience of similar situations or persons with whom you have interacted	22
I make a fresh start of activating all my senses assuming that every person and every situation is different	22
I make a fresh start of activating all my senses assuming that every person and every situation is different, but also recall my experience to validate my understanding	53
Other	3

The answers: Let us classify the respondents in four categories again—A. Those overtly confident about relying on what and how they need to assess. B. Those that are not confident about relying on their past experi-ence and wish to make a fresh assessment C. Those who wish to add value to their experiential data and wish to be qualitatively more accurate with

- Experience of similar situations
  or persons with whom you
  have interacted

- I make a fresh start of
  Actioning all my senses
  Assuming that every person
  And every situation is different

- I make a fresh start of
  actioning all my senses
  assuming that every person
  and every situation is different,
  but also recall my experience
  to validate my understanding

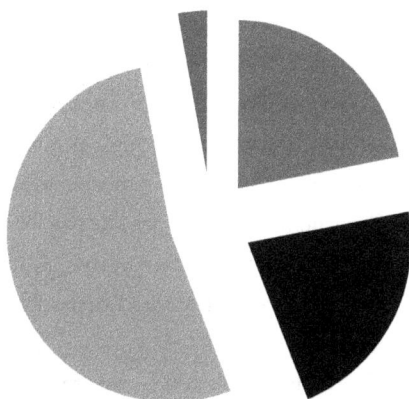

- Other

their assessments and D. Those, who do not comprehend, the direction in which, the question is trying to probe.

(A) is a group of 22 percent persons who fundamentally do not question their experience. Why they seemingly appear to be overconfident is perhaps, because, they are largely overlooking the fact that with the passage of time, when there is a likelihood of contextual change, the responses also are likely to be different in more than one way. (B) This is a group that does not wish to rely on earlier experience and wish to make observations afresh to make its assessments, even though those in that group might have had similar experiences. Perhaps they do not trust their data recall. They too are 22 percent of the sample surveyed. (C) Those in this group (53 percent) are "aware" that their assessments based on their experiences, no doubt would be an active and valid input but such inputs need to be validated further as contexts keep changing much faster today than it ever did before. They are conscious of the quality of the assessment to be made, while maintaining the contemporariness of the situation or the person. Analyzing the responses in (D) would not bear any fruit (only 3 percent) in the midst of our background of discussions here. The most rational response is from (C). Let us understand this with an illustration cited earlier.

Martin Wickramasinghe, the historian, social anthropologist and writer from Sri Lanka, whose biography has been discussed in brief, in our earlier pages, stands out to exemplify what is being stated here. Wickramasinghe started his journalistic career in "Dinamina" in 1916 and after having spent five years in the organization was elevated to the editorial staff in 1921, when he also got married. He left the organization to join "Lakmina" in 1927. This meant that he had good 11 years of rich experience in "Dinamina," enough to create influential perceptions about people and subjects that the paper covered. But we notice that when he returned to the paper five years later as the editor of this Sinhala national daily, he had a different perspective. A fairly large chunk of time had lapsed, since he had last worked there. Times had changed and the context had changed.

Dr. S. Radhakrishnan, the great teacher and philosopher had summarized it all when he frequently quoted Confucius (as already cited in the chapter denoting perceptiveness of teachers), "He who by re-animating the Old can gain knowledge of the New is fit to be a teacher." He had certainly said so in reference to the teaching profession, where the characteristic of understanding plays an extremely vital role. In contemporary language, let us put it this way. Visit your repository of knowledge to understand and comprehend a situation or a person but do not withhold yourself to acquire the new, to validate your data.

Cecil B. DeMille not only while making The 10 Commandments, visited and revisited issues and approaches with a different perspective every time, but also as must have been noticed his tendencies of upgrading his perception with changing times has been astounding. At the cost of repeating, the following statement has been reproduced about him. "The arrival of the "talkies" did not deter the resolve that Cecil had. His resilience assisted him to transition his approach. He even devised a microphone boom, a soundproof camera blimp [housing] and also popularized the camera crane."

The Seventh Question: *Do you make serious efforts to find out how your behavior has been viewed by the person with whom you have been interacting?*

The explanation: Even a toddler looks for acknowledgement of behavior… a nod, a smile, a hug, a frown or a glaring eye! His behavior is thereafter reinforced accordingly. Every communication would be incomplete if a feedback is not received. The good old theories in communication have been publicizing since time immemorial, about feedback. But it is interesting to see that it is not whole heartedly practiced even then. The westerners generally are a little more conscious about a candid response than their Asian counterparts. The response need not be a feedback with clarity though. Providing a feedback with clarity is a skill only a few possess. Usually those who are espousing or awaiting a feedback, are responsibly expected to comprehend the response on their own, through their perceptions of anything that prevails between body language and total silence (a conventional means of response in eastern and southern Asia that could be again interpreted in a variety of ways—anything from joy to acceptance to fury), past validated interpretations, the contextual facts or further tactful probes. They are aware that the feedback on its own was a farfetched expectation and therefore the idea of this effort. Incidentally, a feedback is a must, whether a deliberate one, which could be voluntary from the respondent's perspective, or an espoused one (involuntary). An espoused feedback would be when the respondent has been able to communicate as an outcome of all the efforts made by the one who is trying to comprehend the response. There are situations or responses where all is left to the one who is trying to understand. Kazi Nazrul Islam, the famous writer had to infer that he was being let down on his promises by his friend A.K. Fazlul Huq when he was working for the paper Daily Nabajug without getting to be told about it, as mentioned in the earlier pages. The reason that a feedback is essential is that comprehension and understanding by the one who has to receive the feedback eventually has to emerge out of the state of "ignorance." In order to stay informed about all that is happening around him, it is a necessity. The urge for understanding therefore has to be intense irrespective of whether the respondent is responding or not. In many cases, situations or events occur where perhaps the expectation to receive any kind of response stands at nil. It is common to see people not replying to your calls, mails or messages. Despite that, the knowledge seeker has to go on.

Answers	Percentage
Yes I do always	36
Yes, only sometimes when I am unsure of the responses	47

Never, I feel it is invading into someone's
privacy   15
Other   2

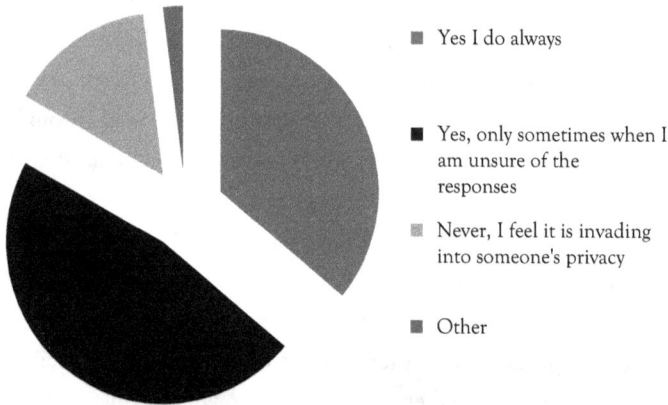

- Yes I do always

- Yes, only sometimes when I am unsure of the responses

- Never, I feel it is invading into someone's privacy

- Other

Answers: We find from the survey carried out that 36 percent wish to ensure a feedback, in whatever form or manner they would get. 47 percent would like to rely on their previous experiences for a surmise of the situation and perhaps would refrain from probing for fresher evidence, unless compelled to, only if the findings were not corroborating with earlier ones. 15 percent would not really bother and would like to remain where they were. Two percent of the population suggested actions which were not relevant in the context being discussed. Let me quote my experience of teaching some post graduate management students. My discovery was that there were five different categories which I had unmindfully constructed. (1) Those from affluent families but were doing the course for a pastime—would eventually finish the course and go back to their family businesses with a stamp of a post graduate management certification. (2) Those from affluent families but were doing the course with a serious intention of applying their learning into their family businesses. (3) Those from not so affluent families and were doing the course with the hope of acquiring a respectable job immediately after the course, but were in a quandary with regard to the opportunities they needed to explore. (4) Those again from not so affluent families and were doing the course with the hope of acquiring a respectable job immediately after the course, but were conversant with the ways of the world and knew what exactly they had to do and then (5) those who had no clue about why they were into a management course—probably the only guideline they had was that this course would fetch them a high priced job. For me teaching was always an interactive process. The process had many advantages but what would be worthwhile mentioning here would be to have a response that brought clarity to my "satisfaction" of having been able to convey. My quest was for making that student understand, who was the poorest in comprehending. The biggest disadvantage was that of the "smarter" students having to bear with my process. But I used to get away, by instilling in them the confidence that these were lessons in patience for their future leadership roles. The gigantic task was to elicit responses to my utterances from categories (1) and (5), in particular. Having been able to do so, there were many conversions into taking interest in the subjects that I taught. The point I wish to make is that educing more information about the communication style and empathizing with the psychosocial status of each of them, acted as a big tool in the formation of the right perceptions. Over a period of time I graduated to a perceptive state when I could mark the attendance in the class, without calling out their names or even looking at them. I could raise my level of perceptiveness by refreshing my repository of perceptions.

The Eighth Question: *Do you carefully observe how a person takes what you tell him/her, and then accordingly communicate?*

The explanation: In fact this question is an extension of the seventh question, but garbed to espouse a validated response, which is evident in the answers. The question is trying to probe the ways and means adopted in eliciting a response. Are you hammering your standard method of extracting information whether the respondent has been able to respond in the way you expected or otherwise? Remember how Akira Kurosawa was unpopular in eliciting a positive response from the Japanese audience in his initial fling with cinema, which was under plenty of American or western influence? His style did not work. Eventually he picked on a unique style, which was a blend of the traditional Japanese theatre of "noh" and "kabuki" and his "western" techniques and shot to become a rage. He had to become popular at home first before launching himself as an international film maker and for that he had to have the right perceptions that worked. His perceptiveness had worked. His wait for the audience response had worked.

The Jio launch in India had to pervade the operational orbit of other well established telecom operators. The edge, that Jio was planned to have, was an exclusive 4G service. Older phones that only supported 3G, was not meant to work. Also it was not supposed to work on feature phones. You needed 4G connectivity. To make calls, Jio was supposed to rely on VoLTE network. This was something new in India. This meant that calls are made using data connection. While it was no problem for Jio to Jio calls. But for the Jio to GSM calls, one had to install an app called Jio Join because the calls would use interconnecting infrastructure that the usual telecom operators used. Even then there was a chance that calls would fail. Reliance CMD Mukesh Ambani himself confessed that in a tried out one week, 5 crore Jio calls failed. Although, he also said in the same breath that existing telecom operators were not doing their bit to make the service good for consumers. Why then was this calculated risk taken? The strategy used was a tactical deliberation to watch out for the response of the prospective customers, (a) posing a serious competition to the existing operators in terms of (i) creating a phenomenally large consumer base and (ii) bringing in a technology that the other operators were hesitant to and (b) foreseeing the future means of operations in consumer telecommunications. Imagine the effort made to probe for a response that would enhance the perception of the organization behind Jio and eventually its perceptiveness. Reliance Jio Infocomm Limited has taken the telecom industry by storm and is awaiting the response from its subscribers and other respondents to calculate its next stroke.

Answers: Only 19.59 percent assertively say that they always waited for the audience response. In other words they were more calculative in placing their next stroke than the others. The next lot

Answers	Percentage
Yes, very clearly	19.59
No, not at all	13.4
To some extent	65.98
Others	1.03

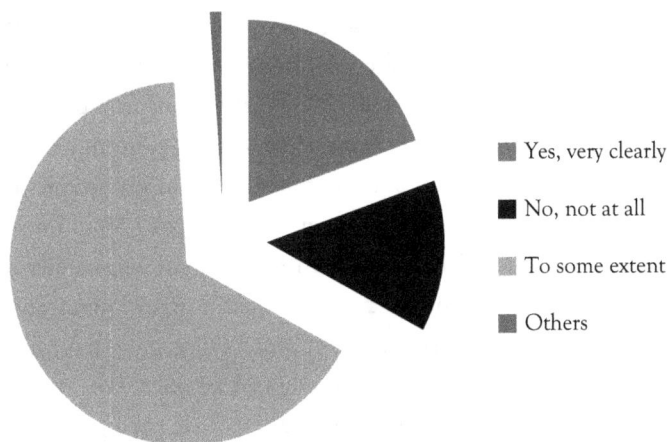

- ■ Yes, very clearly
- ■ No, not at all
- ■ To some extent
- ■ Others

appears to be more reactive or perhaps less calculative (13.4 percent). Their next stroke would mean that either they would not react or perhaps would tend to respond immediately, based on their past experience. The 65.98 percent is the vast majority that would either await the response or may even respond immediately depending on the situation or the person. That is, in some cases one would feel not so confident about the response and would like to wait and check, whilst in some others, one felt convinced, that their interpretation of the responses based on their earlier experiences would be by and large correct. It was only 1.03 percent respondents whose answers were irrelevant. Yes, come to think of it, most of us fall in the third category, where we do not wish to check for fresh substantiation and do not wait to watch with patience the forthcoming responses. I knew one Shankar, who was into a catering business and was earning good sums of money during the "marriage seasons" by serving choicest delicacies at dinner and tea parties during those days. Marriages and weddings in India are ceremoniously embedded with lavish dinners or tea parties. Again most of the marriages take place during certain times of the year amongst the majority. Shankar had been planning to visit his aged mother living all by herself in a remote village far away. Once he chose to give fulfillment to his long standing desire during the "off season" in the Indian month of *Pausa* (January), during which month, the majority tends to avoid fixing dates for weddings. He booked his railway tickets at least a month or so in advance. A friend of his called him in the third week of December only to tell him that there was a wealthy Christian family who was organizing their daughter's wedding in January at Jaipur. They were essentially hunting for Shankar knowing his reputation about the quality of food that he served. They were looking at a three to four day event that included *sagai* (engagement), *mehndi* (adorning the henna motifs), *vivah* (the wedding) and the reception from the groom's family and Shankar was to organize food for guests numbering 50 to three hundred on each occasion. They were keen to have only one caterer for all the four days. It was no doubt a phenomenal business opportunity for Shankar. His taking up the offer meant proliferating growth for his business, as this family was one that was counted amongst the "connected" people. Also the prospective customers not only were paying a better price than Shankar usually fetched but also were paying for travel and stay of his catering team as well. Secondly the "word of mouth" is what builds a brand for this kind of business. Shankar's trip to his village had to be postponed indefinitely and he could make a quick round only six months later. Looking at this instance we find that Shankar was relying on his past experience of a lean period in January and had not refreshed his data bank of market information on opportunities…his friends and contacts and as to what kind of opportunities they could provide. His idea of responses had become outdated, which is why his plan for a vacation went awry.

The Ninth Question: *Do you tend to categorize people and situations in terms of your previous assessments of similar nature and frame them thus?*

The explanation: Again, this is an extension of, or carrying forward the probe with regard to the previous two questions. But this is also a clue to finding out as to how biases get generated. No doubt such a situation would occur when you have stretched your categories too far without updating your information bank. It would not be out of place to see a continuum with two extremes.

[X] Being perceptive		[Y] Being biased

In other words, two kinds of extreme circumstances are seen. [X] is a circumstance where the observer has been seriously pursuing to update his knowledge about a person or a situation, either out of direct interest or compulsive curiosity. And therefore is able to correctly perceive consequences, even without having to probe much. The observer is called perceptive. [Y] is a condition, which arises out of your understanding of a person or a situation without updating your knowledge of the facts about them or because of relying on out dated information. Such an observer would be termed as dogmatic, biased or prejudiced.

Without further building on this correlation and leaving it aside for more elaborate discussions elsewhere and another time, let us go on to discussing the point that needs to be highlighted. That is the structuring of categories or types in our minds and what play into building them. We have already seen in the First Question the following, "Based on one's observations of a person's behavioral responses to situations and behavior one has to use his/her alertness to comprehend the pattern." In this portion let us dwell on the variables that determine the comprehension. There are two parts to this. One part is entirely dependent on the facts observed. The behavior observed and encoded as a response to the causes recorded. The other part is the interpretation of the behavioral response in the context, giving rise to an understanding, which in turn depends on the psycho-social perspective of the observer, and how well that has been validated. The geographical location, the culture of the hinterland, the right understanding of the colloquial usage and the "neutrality or happiness—count" of the observer are the most prominent variables. This perspective is extremely significant for the correctness of the understanding. The absence or aberration of any of variables or their comprehension can jeopardize the accuracy of the conception of the category or type in which one would frame the subject—whether an individual or a situation. (Or push you toward a prejudiced understanding!)

Answers	Percentage
Yes mostly, unless I find something remarkably different	37
Sometimes, when I begin to find identical attributes	54
Never	12
Others	0

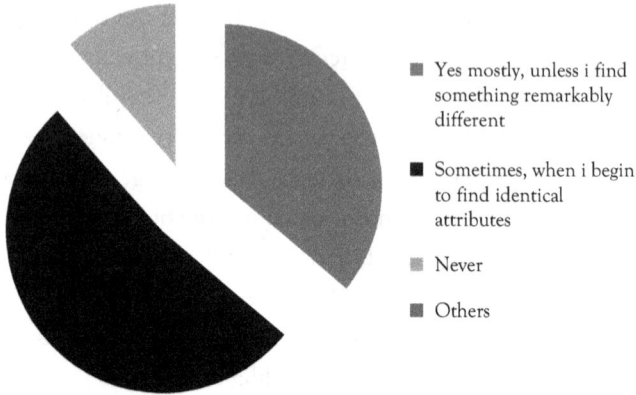

- Yes mostly, unless i find something remarkably different
- Sometimes, when i begin to find identical attributes
- Never
- Others

Answers: There were respondents amongst the audience surveyed, who confessed that they do not check back unless something different apparently shows up. Thirty-seven percent of the population surveyed communicated thus, vouching for not realizing the need to check up on the behavioral updates, regularly. An update becomes necessary, when one is startled to see an astonishingly different response or responses. Deveshwar had been employed with a small company for more than seven years. He and his employer Naresh shared a very cordial relationship. Naresh knew every time as to what Deveshwar aspired for and how he needed a support from the company in terms of financial assistance. Naresh also knew Deveshwar's inherent interests in technology. He relished every work that was technical in nature. Naresh was planning to allot him a technical role in his new project which was on the anvil. In the meanwhile, Deveshwar had also picked up some basic skills in accountancy. While Naresh knew that he was involved in book writing he had not checked of late, if he found that work interesting and was assuming that he found it boring, which he did, when he was initially allocated that work. Therefore, Deveshwar's refusal to move out for the new role, when the launch of the new project matured, came to him as a shock. 54 percent respondents confirmed that categorizing persons or situations was a normal trend and that they did so, when they found repeated consistency in behavioral responses. Satyajit Ray had in the assessment of his own self made different moves in life, just as Martin Wickramasinghe did, but distinctly his passion in making films stood out even for others to see. He had no doubt inherited the family skills in printing and later in writing followed by calligraphy and design.

His skills in writing brought him closer to films when he started pursuing writing scripts for films. The fire in him for making films was kindled by his senior colleague D. K. Gupta with his suggestion to make the film "Pather Panchali" and his becoming aware of film-making with amateur artists after having watched the film, "Bicycle Thieves" in London. This illustrates the fact that he was categorized into a film-maker and every step or action that he took (the behavioral responses that he displayed) brought him closer to being bracketed as one. Wickramasinghe on the other hand came closer to his becoming a legendary historian in the region. In both the illustrations one would discover different behavioral responses but each one was pushing the belief to coming one step closer to the core area of excellence. There was a consistency in the moves and thus the categorization that emerged. There was a group of 12 percent of the respondents who confessed that they never derived any category and every time made a fresh assessment of the person or the situation. This has to be taken with a pinch of salt because it has been experienced that observers *do* judge a person or a situation and one would find it difficult to create an impression about or judging what one is observing without letting earlier impressions and thoughts influencing your present. It is possible that they might not have formally categorized or typed or given it a name, but previous images do linger. Having to believe what these respondents have stated we can only comment that either they have been able to work on themselves commendably to be able to start on a white sheet or are not clear or have not analyzed their approach well.

The Tenth Question: *Which of the following personality attributes describes you best?*

The explanation: This question was asked only to ensure if there was a correlation between perceptiveness and the character types—Analytical, Expressive, Empathic and Driver. These character types are not a depiction of such characters prevailing in exclusivity in a person. All these characters are prevalent in every human being. It is only that one character dominates the others. The domination of one character is observed in most situations and accordingly an individual is grouped. Usually the dominant character is backed up by another. Therefore an individual is usually guided by two main forms of character—the dominant character/style and the back-up character/style. The correlation between perceptiveness and any of the four styles is as difficult to establish as it is to confirm that in a particular situation an individual response would be predominantly governed by one character. In the effort to exemplify the expression of perceptiveness through writers, teachers and those who aspired to be an auteur, the challenge has been to highlight all factual happenings and identify those that exhibited their perceptiveness, as we have learnt to recognize it. Let us examine in detail the attributes of each of these characters/styles (thanks to persuasive.net).

Analytical

- Sees overt emotion as a weakness and something to distrust.
- Needs facts, numbers, and details. Will seek out more information.
- Usually known for being a perfectionist, hates to make errors. Doesn't forgive mistakes easily in themselves or others. Seen as intolerant.
- Great problem solving skills. Wants to be admired for their problem solving abilities.
- Likes organization and structure. Will sometimes hold to "rules" even when results suffer.
- Soft voice, reserved. Not directly confrontational. Lets the data speak for itself. Expects others to agree based on facts and logical arguments.
- Gets frustrated when people don't see "the right answer" as clearly as they do.
- Usually doesn't get bored—internal life (thinking about "stuff") keeps them occupied when outside stimulus is low.

What should catch our attention is the reliance on data?

Driver

- Demands control or will take it when available. Looks for opportunity to be "in charge."

- Will get things done, likes goals and achieving them. Frames life as a sequence of I did this.
- Straight to the point, looks for the bottom line. Dislikes complexity or ambiguity.
- Little patience for the small details that aren't clearly in line with goal seeking.
- Doesn't like situations where they have no say in what's happening.
- Appears to be arrogant and standoffish. Can seem overly aggressive, especially in the heat of a project. Will see people as "obstacles" or "allies."
- Can appear to be very confident

Expressive

- Tends to run late, lots of commitments and rushed lifestyle.
- Desires to be centre of attention. Will attempt to draw focus of a group.
- Can't stand being bored, impatient. Will get stressed and fidget in lines, looks for distractions.
- Generally have brightly colored clothing/cars/houses. Values "flash."
- They are animated and lively when they speak or tell stories. Sometimes seem "loud."

Amiable

- Team player, looks for an "everybody wins" result.
- Warm and friendly, but sometimes cloying.
- Doesn't hide from feelings, expressing and listening. Caring, nurturing come easily.
- Soft spoken, goes along to "get along." Uncomfortable when they don't know how the group feels about something. Doesn't like independent activities and decision making.
- Rarely sticks up for their position in the face of strong opposition. Prefers compromise.

I have intentionally not sought a correlation with the MBTI types because the understanding is that a perceptive person could be extrovert or an introvert. Likewise he could be intuitive, or sensing, or thinking or feeling. In other words, the cognitive elements would always work at their best and it is not significant therefore, to identify which (combination) type is more perceptive.

An inventory based Psychometric test that determines your "dominant" style and your "back-up" style of functioning, in terms of the previous classification.

My Style

Consider each of the following questions separately and circle the one letter (a, b, c, or d) that corresponds to the description which fits your most. If you have trouble in selecting any one answer, select the one, which responds at work that would be the most natural or likely option for you to take.

1. When talking to a person during the meeting…
    (a) I maintain eye contact the whole time
    (b) I alternate between looking at the person and looking down
    (c) I look around the room a good deal of the time
    (d) I try to maintain eye contact but look away from time to time.
2. When I have a decision to make about a person…
    (a) I think it through completely before deciding
    (b) I go with my gut instincts
    (c) I consider the impact it will have on other people before deciding
    (d) I run it by someone whose opinion I respect before deciding
3. I like to have the meeting room with…
    (a) My team photos and sentimental items displayed
    (b) Inspirational posters, awards and art displayed
    (c) Graphs and charts displayed
    (d) Calendars and project outlines displayed
4. If I am having a conflict with a meeting partner…
    (a) I try to help the situation along by focusing on the positive
    (b) I stay calm and try to understand the cause of the conflict
    (c) I try to avoid discussing the issue causing the conflict

(d) I confront it right away so that it can get resolved as soon as possible

5. When I am meeting on the phone ...
   (a) I keep the conversation focused on the purpose of the call
   (b) I will spend a few minutes chatting before getting down to business
   (c) I am in no hurry to get off the phone and do not mind chatting about personal things, the weather, and so on.
   (d) I try to keep the conversation as brief as possible.

6. If a person is upset...
   (a) I ask if I can do anything to help
   (b) I leave him alone because I do not want to intrude on his privacy
   (c) I try to cheer him up and help him to see the bright side
   (d) I feel uncomfortable and hope he gets over it soon

7. When I conduct meetings...
   (a) I sit back and think about what is being said before offering my opinion
   (b) I put all my cards on the table so my opinion is well known
   (c) I express my opinion enthusiastically, but listen to other's ideas as well
   (d) I try to support the ideas of the other people in the meeting.

8. When I speak to the persons ...
   (a) I am entertaining and often humorous
   (b) I am clear and concise
   (c) I speak relatively quietly
   (d) I am direct, specific, and sometimes loud.

9. When a person is explaining a problem to me...
   (a) I try to understand and empathize with how he/she is feeling
   (b) I look for the specific facts pertaining to the situation
   (c) I listen carefully for the main issue so that I can find a solution
   (d) I use my body language and tone of voice to show him/her that I understand

10. When I listen to a person...
    (a) I get bored if the person moves too slowly
    (b) I try to be supportive of the person, knowing how hard it is
    (c) I want it to be a entertaining as well as informative
    (d) I look for the logic behind what the person is saying

11. When I want to get my point across to persons...
    (a) I listen to their point of view first and then express my ideas gently
    (b) I strongly state my opinion so that they know where I stand
    (c) I try to persuade them without being too forceful
    (d) I explain the thinking and logic behind what I am saying.

12. When I am late for a meeting...
    (a) I do not panic but call up to inform the persons that I will be a few minutes late
    (b) I feel bad about keeping the persons waiting
    (c) I get very upset and rush to get there as soon as possible
    (d) I apologize profusely once I arrive.

13. I like the persons to set goals and objectives at work that...
    (a) They think they can realistically attain
    (b) They feel are challenging and would be exciting to achieve
    (c) They need to achieve as part of a bigger objective
    (d) Will make them feel good when they achieve those

14. When explaining a problem to a person whom I need response from...
    (a) I explain the problem in as much detail as possible
    (b) I sometimes exaggerate to make my point
    (c) I try to explain how the problem makes me feel
    (d) I explain how I would like the problem to be solved.

15. If persons are late for an meeting ...
    (a) I keep myself busy by making phone calls or working until they arrive.
    (b) I assume they were delayed a bit and do not get upset
    (c) I call to make sure that I have the correct information (date, time, and so on).
    (d) I get upset that the person is wasting my time.

16. When I am behind on a project and feel pressure to get it done...
    (a) I make a list everything I need to do, in what order, by when.
    (b) I block out everything else and focus 100 percent on the work I need to do
    (c) I become anxious and have a hard time focusing on my work
    (d) I set a date to get the project done by and go for it.

17. When I feel the person's behavior to be too aggressive…

   (a) I tell him/her to stop it

   (b) I feel hurt but usually do not say anything about it to him/her

   (c) I ignore his/her anger and try to focus on the facts of the situation

   (d) I let him/her know in strong terms that I do not like his/her behavior

18. When I see a person for the first time…

   (a) I give him a friendly smile

   (b) I greet him but do not shake his hand

   (c) I give him a firm but quick handshake

   (d) I give him an enthusiastic handshake that lasts fee moments.

My Styles—Scoring Form

1 a. Driver b. Amiable c. Analytical d. Expressive	**7** a. Analytical b. Driver c. Expressive d. Amiable	**13** a. Analytical b. Expressive c. Driver d. Amiable
2 a. Analytical b. Driver c. Amiable d. Expressive	**8** a. Expressive b. Analytical c. Amiable d. Driver	**14** a. Analytical b. Expressive c. Amiable d. Driver
3 a. Amiable b. Expressive c. Analytical d. Driver	**9** a. Amiable b. Analytical c. Driver d. Expressive	**15** a. Expressive b. Amiable c. Analytical d. Driver
4 a. Expressive b. Amiable c. Analytical d. Driver	**10** a. Driver b. Amiable c. Expressive d. Analytical	**16** a. Analytical b. Driver c. Amiable d. Expressive
5 a. Driver b. Expressive c. Amiable d. Analytical	**11** a. Amiable b. Driver c. Expressive d. Analytical	**17** a. Driver b. Amiable c. Analytical d. Expressive
6 a. Amiable b. Analytical c. Expressive d. Driver	**12** a. Analytical b. Amiable c. Driver d. Expressive	**18** a. Amiable b. Analytical c. Driver d. Expressive

Count the number of "analyticals," "amiables," "drivers," and "expressives." Whatever is the highest score is your dominant style and your second highest score is your backup style.

Here are some of the typical attributes of workplace behavior that each style would go to show. (What is seen as follows is researched work that is available and is not a fresh conclusion.)

Mode of behavior	Analytical	Driver	Amiable	Expressive
On the telephone	Fairly short. Gives you all the details	Short. Tells purpose and hangs up	Medium length. Shares everything with you and want you to do the same	Lengthy. Can and will talk about anything and everything
Expects	To give facts and make sure they are true	To give results. Use caution and let him/her be in charge	To be her/his friend and handle her/his problems	To let her/him feel accepted. A part of the problem solving process
Thinks in	Present	Here and now	Past	Future
Ask how are they	Think, based on their own analysis	React to main point	Feel you are tracking with them	Feel about the concept
Backup your decision with	Evidence	Options	Assurances	Incentives
At their best	Deliberate Prudent Objective Rational	Assertive Objective Confident Competitive	Spontaneous Persuasive Empathetic Loyal	Original Imaginative Creative Idealistic
At their worst	Talkative Rigid Indecisive Over cautious	Arrogant Domineering Untrusting Self-Involvement	Impulsive Manipulative Subjective Sentimental	Unrealistic Impractical Out of touch Devious

The test and the inferences have been provided here to communicate an understanding and also the feel as to what each character would actually display.

The responses to the survey stand out as follows:

Answer	Percentage
Analytical	48
Expressive	40
Empathic (Amiable)	36
Driver	13

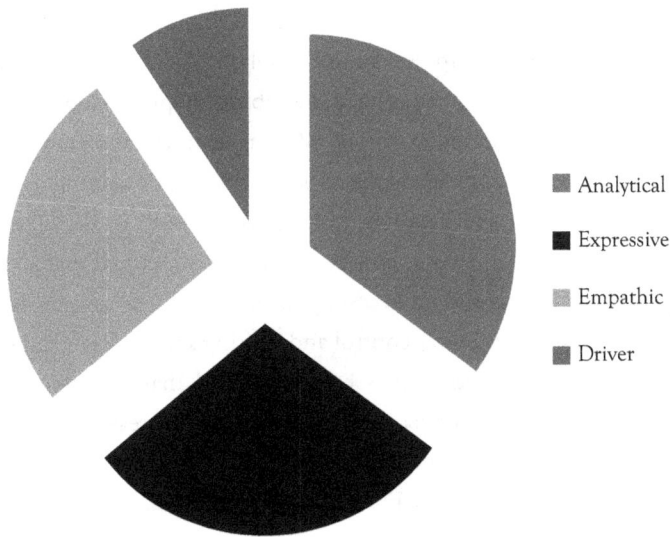

Analytical

Expressive

Empathic

Driver

The Answers: The correlation between the character types and perceptiveness has been observed and summarized on the basis of trends in social behavior. Recently a group of 3,425 students studying in the fifth to the ninth standards in Munich, Germany were surveyed. https://eurekalert.org/pub_releases/2012-12/sfri-msh121312.php Dr. Kou Murayama, postdoctoral researcher of psychology at the University of California, Los Angeles (who was then at the University of Munich) led the study. Dr. Murayama's research draws on broad psychological theories regarding motivation and cognition from the neural level to the social level. Specific topics of interest include motivation and memory, motivation and metacognition, the nature and consequence of competition, the nature of intrinsic motivation/curiosity. The study that is being referred to here, infers greater success in life of students, who were found good in their mathematical abilities. If we scrutinize what these abilities more closely we would find much more. Most researchers agree that memory, language, attention, temporal-sequential ordering, higher-order cognition, and spatial ordering are among the neuro-developmental functions that play a role when children think with numbers. These components become part of an ongoing process in which children constantly integrate new concepts and procedural skills as they solve more advanced math problems. This competence draws on more than just the ability to calculate answers efficiently. It also encompasses problem solving, communicating about mathematical concepts, reasoning and establishing proof, and representing information in different forms. Making connections among these skills and concepts both in mathematics and in other subjects is something students are more frequently asked to do, both in the classroom setting, and later in the workplace. Research has established that a variety of general cognitive skills are necessary for mathematical success, such as working memory, inhibitory control and shifting skills (Cragg and Gilmore 2014). More recently it has been suggested that logical reasoning skills are an important aspect of good mathematical reasoning abilities. Analytical ability is fundamentally utilized to solve problems and that is exactly what we do in mathematics—solve problems. Problems outside mathematics need to be understood in the context of the process that has led to the problem. The analyst breaks down the process and identifies the facts that have built the process leading to the problem. In mathematics we examine the figures in the problem and the connectivity between them, in terms of addition, subtraction, multiplication or division that determine the process in leading to the problem. This goes to show the parity between the two. The next question that we need to ask ourselves is whether our analytical ability is a tool that enhances our perceptiveness. If we pore over our understanding of perceptiveness once again, it would reveal the following steps in cultivating the attribute.

1. Remaining alert to our surroundings
2. Generating curiosity to know more
3. Observing carefully the visible facts
4. Probing to grasp the invisible facts
5. Comprehending the facts in the appropriate contextual perspective
6. Arriving at an understanding/comprehension

Let us examine one by one. What characteristic of ours would prompt us to remain alert? Health experts have so far been able to identify only factors that energize or dampen one's alertness but not been able to explain what generates it. Therefore alertness is as fundamental an attribute that a living being possesses given the use of senses. I have been able to spot a few "additives" and "sedatives," which are self explanatory.

> *Overstimulation*—The brain can only take in so much at one time, at some point it just shuts down and says "Enough!" When too much is going on around you, whether it is a busy day at work or the kids are driving you stark, raving mad, simply step back a few minutes and find a quiet place to relax. There are several 10 min guided meditations that are designed to help you shut out the world and find a quiet place within in order to clear your mind of all the chaos. You'd be amazed at what "centering" meditations can do to clear your mind and restore mental alertness!
>
> *Metal/Chemical Toxicity*—Copper, cadmium, mercury, calcium, zinc, lead, and aluminum are quite often at toxic levels in the body and do, in fact, adversely affect mental acuity. Unfortunately, a simple blood test will not usually reveal toxic levels of minerals in the body so it may be necessary to check out Chelation therapy and go onto something known as a Slow Oxidizer Diet. Chelation therapy uses compounds that pick up toxic minerals in the blood stream by bonding with them in order to render them harmless for removal and the Slow Oxidizer Diet by Lawrence Wilson, M.D. provides dietary means of removing toxic levels of chemicals.
>
> *Irregularity/Toxic Bowels*—Foods that have not been properly digested can slowly putrefy breeding toxins which build up in the liver and other organs, including the brain. Not only do you feel sluggish mentally, but also a toxic colon can also keep you from optimal performance physically as well. Adding high fiber foods to your diet such as whole grains can help, but many people find the need to take a colon cleansing supplement as well. Once the intestines are flushed of a toxic build-up, most people report feeling almost imme-diately invigorated. However, some colon cleansing supplements on the market are not as safe as they should be and it is recommended

that products containing *cascara sagrada* be avoided as they are too harsh for most people.

Electromagnetic Toxicity—Common sources are computer screens, cell phones, electrical wiring in buildings, cell phone towers and high voltage power neighborhood distribution lines. This is another cause for concern which most of us are plagued by. If you live more than 300 feet from those high voltage power lines you are probably at a safe distance, however it is more difficult to stay away from the electromagnetic fields (EMF) from cell phones and computer monitors. It is suggested that you use a headset for your phone and stay a safe distance from your computer when working on it. These are luxuries of the modern technological age, but they can wreak havoc in other areas of our lives.

Hypoglycemia—Low levels of blood sugar deprive the brain of energy. The easiest way to remedy low blood sugar when you feel like you are sapped of energy and simply unable to focus is to heat a complex carbohydrate energy bar. Fresh fruits are also ideal for providing a quick burst of energy when your blood sugar levels have bottomed out. Unfortunately, most people grab a quick cup of coffee which just exacerbates the problem because caffeine tends to burn what little blood sugar you have left too quickly. Complex carbohydrates work best.

Nutritional Deficiencies and Allergies—Another of the major reasons why many people lack mental alertness is diet, either allergies to foods they are eating or inadequate nutrients in overprocessed foods. If you don't have the resources to have yourself tested for food allergies by a medical doctor, then the best method is to eliminate certain of the major culprits from your diet, one by one. There is a lot of information on this method available and it might be you can find the food or foods that are causing you distress. Nutritional deficiencies are often easier to correct with a balanced diet of healthy whole foods and/or a vitamin and mineral supplement daily.

These implements, as can be observed, only work as catalysts and can be monitored to address the first step observed in crafting and instilling perceptiveness, but nothing beyond.

An analytical person has the element: (a) Needs facts, numbers, and details. (b) Will seek out more information. These features are imminent when one wants to know or keen to learn and therefore constitute the essentials of the second step.

Similarly the need to observe facts is essential in order to understand them. The old habit of taking down notes on what you have observed or in today's times the habit of taking pictures. What are we trying to do? Keep record of what we have observed, while minimizing the chance of letting facts slip out from memory and creating a reference point. Being observant means watching people, situations, and events, then thinking critically about what you see. Manish Chopra, a principal with McKinsey & Company states that Vipassana, an ancient form of meditation having its roots in the subcontinent, he felt, has augmented his ability to observe. I personally think any form of meditation raises one's concentration and focus levels. Thorin Klosowski, a blogger at "Lifehacker" writes that it was impossible to observe everything and therefore you have to train your mind as to what your priorities were and further train to observe what you wish to. It is imperative therefore while agreeing with both of them that in order to be a great observer, one needs to have variant exposure, which is significantly as important as exercising—both physical and metaphysical. Robin Sharma the famous coach and trainer also emphasizes the need for exercising in discovering one's personal potential. The connection between observation and the personality types as seen earlier, is more of a simple deduction, than anything else; they were the areas of interest that subscribe enormously to what one observes. Areas of interest may vary considerably with the personality type. But it goes without elaborating further that the analytical ability is a must. If one looks at the fourth, the fifth and the sixth steps (probing to grasp the invisible facts—comprehending the facts in the appropriate contextual perspective—arriving at an understanding/comprehension) they are all actions generated by the analytical ability in a person—whether one is predominantly expressive, or amiable or even a driver, the analytical element is a must for a majority of the measures needed to be perceptive.

Conclusions of the Chapter: Figuratively these empirical studies promise us that a significant factor in our behavior that chips in to steer

our way through challenges in the contemporary world is perceptiveness. In addition, they also stake their claim on what is needed
to build perceptiveness. Curiosity to not only know but also to
know more is a fundamental quality that emerges as a contributory
factor. The perspective of being alert has to be formidably realized
as the flow of information is humungous and there is every reason
to be far more vigilant than what it was only 10 years ago. Every
piece of information matters for it creates a ripple that touches
another, even though peripherally. If Tesla has evolved a method of
wireless charging scores of gadgets simultaneously does it not affect
the future of the dependability on electronic communication at
anytime—in warfare and in times of peace? Can you think of the
pace at which gadgets would recoup and diminish their standby
time? The next learning is that the fundamentals of superficiality
would always be questioned with enhanced perceptiveness, for the
inclination to probe and continue to probe is an essential ingredi-
ent that we have come to realize through these investigations. The
tenacity and the patience needed for observations have also surfaced
as a "by-product" finding and it would not be justifiably asserted
by simply saying so, but has to be realized as an essential constituent. Getting to know the pattern of responses in given situations
is the key to perceptiveness. The risk of depending exclusively on
past responses, however, is a factor that cannot be ignored by any
means. Alertness once again pays its dividend and one needs to
review the responses in their contemporary perspective. This may
direct you to comprehend it as a deviation from the usual responses
or it may reinforce and reinstate your previous understanding. If
deviations are observed, they might have to be seen in the light of
the changed physical or social environment or the contemporary
perspective, the pros and cons of which need to be analyzed in
detail, before a conclusive inference is made.

I wonder if you noticed that unbiased (open), sharp (accurate and
validated) and profound (in-depth) perception skills are the window to
perceptiveness.

Lessons for Contemporary Management Thought

Traditionally management speaks of how systems, methods, equipment, processes, resources including people are run in an organization to attain the organizational goals. Although a very simplistic definition, it is definitely all encompassing. I am of the firm opinion that however aggressively automated, may your core functionalities be, the human element cannot be discarded. Dave Ulrich, the contemporary human resource management guru of this century, who has been primarily instrumental in revolutionizing the approach in human resource management, in one of his early works, "Organizational Capability" affirms, without mincing words, that despite tweaking all other resources lead to a competitive advantage, they do so only transitorily. It is only development of its human resources that would not only drive the organization toward its competitive advantage, which would eventually come to stay, but also raise its capability maturity. This postulate is universally proven. To muster and master other resources, the role of human resources is inevitable and once your "learned" human resources are motivated to continually learn and develop, scanning, identifying and positioning other resources, becomes a smooth task. This is to substantiate the significance of human beings in organizations vis-à-vis other resources.

Having said that, it must be clarified that the roles, which human beings perform, are broadly classified into two—the operational and the managerial. In the context of what we are discussing in this book, that is, perceptiveness, the meaningfulness is well laid out in both the roles. Let us examine how.

Role of Perceptiveness in Operational Tasks

It cannot be denied that all operational roles are predominantly skill oriented, whether they are skills of the hands or fingers, the dexterities of running machines or use of tools and implements, the presentation skills or the communication skills for selling, or for that matter even the programming skills needed in building software applications. Perceptiveness goes to help them learn or improvise their skills. It also helps in engendering the quality needed for the goods or service produced. In addition, perceptiveness determines the cautiousness toward safety in carrying out the operations. We cannot overlook the fact that all the aforementioned skills contribute significantly toward productivity. Let us examine each process, one by one.

1. *Learning or improvising skills*

We all know that skills are *learnt* through practice and experience, whether they be attained through structurally designed curriculum or through on the job training. When a question is asked, about some picking up the skills faster than the others, we attribute it to aptitude, which in turn is linked to intelligence and talent—inborn and inherent qualities. Let's take the example of singing, which is accepted as an inborn talent. Not everyone can sing. That is true. However, a person who is rendering a song is able to sing it correctly without even following the notations, because he or she has been perceptive to the notes of what he or she has originally heard and has been able to internalize them by practice without a formal training. Then there are others who would do the same, by following the prescribed notations, having been trained in music. Sometimes you would amazingly notice that the quality of rendition of the former is superior. Why does it happen? It could be the texture of the voice or the passion with which it is rendered. Assuming also with all these are at par, haven't you noticed the distinctive mark of the untrained one? In work-life too this is more frequently noticed. An Industrial Training Institute trained machinist and another who has not been as fortunate, operate the lathe in the same workplace, but the latter with distinct precision. These examples point to the quality of assimilation of skills and their display. If we are to peer into what helps in assimilation one of the primary factors undoubtedly is perceptiveness. The higher the perceptiveness the quicker is the grasp and understanding. Translation of the understanding into demonstration and display however, would depend on the quality of practice. The same theory is finitely observable in *improvisation* of skills as well. A machine operator of a strawboard making machine needs to just grasp the improvised skills of a high speed paper making machine operator. As a plant HR executive, many years ago, I had personally ensured the upgrading of skills of operators of age old cylinder mould board making machinery for the operation of the then freshly erected and installed high speed kraft (brown) paper making machinery. Of course not all were eligible for such training. The ones with quicker comprehending abilities were the first choice. What has left an indelible mark in my mind is the handful amongst them who would spend their break time or lunch time observing from a distance the new machine work. Since the lunch time was staggered they had the advantage of doing so. Remarkable adjustment and ability to upscale skills were displayed. Only a period of three months was given and they were there!

An old strawboard making Fourdrinier machine

What these boys did was to emulate the working pattern of their on-the-job trainers and that was no mean task, considering the deadlines allocated and the machine being electronically controlled (thyristor operated), whilst their erstwhile workplace demanded phenomenally slower responses. Their ability to adjust was only a resultant of their induced perceptiveness. They did not lose any

opportunity to imbibe whatever they could without having to moti-
vate them. Their actions spoke about their zeal, even before they
knew they would at one point in time work on this new machine.

2. *Engendering quality*

Precision as per the parameters set by the customer is quality. We
have terms such as "customer satisfaction" and "customer delight"
emanating out of this understanding. Does this mean that the product or service without any form of deviation that would be satisfying
the customer? Or wouldn't it? It all depends on the expectation the
customer has. If it's a product or a service that is delivered to the tee
in conformance to the formal agreement that has been worked out
between the customer and the supplier, we should term that as customer satisfaction. In fact chances of confusion, betrayal and non-
conformance are hugely possible where the expectations have been
vaguely communicated and that too only verbally. Quality assurance
to the customer is an outcome of an "eye for detail" by the supplier
or his team and this is where perceptiveness comes in, even if the
expectations are well documented. If the latter is well conversant
with the expectations of the former by previous experience or by
making that extra effort beyond the briefing (done already by the
leader) to learn more about the customer and his use for the product
or service, it would help him conceive the kind of efforts to bring in
the sort of precision needed. Here's an operator working on a grinding machine that polishes the balls, which eventually would get fitted
as wheels for a rotating office chair. Now if the office chair is for a
factory office the inputs would vary. Therefore the understanding
would not be to focus on the aesthetics, but on characteristics such
as ruggedness and sustainability, as the product would be subjected
to frequent rough use. On the other hand, if it was for a plush corporate office, the looks would be of primary importance. While the
quality parameters vary, the perceptiveness of the machinist would
lead him to a state of comprehension that would inspire him further
to put in the right or accurate inputs. Coming to the second part,
that is, customer delight, which is universally seen as having the following ingredients, is a step ahead. If the treading wheels of the chair
were well lubricated or greased and the surface made extra smooth

the maneuverability of the chair would be easier than expected the supplier is providing a customer delight. The ingredients of customer delight: (1) The customer gets bowled over. (2) Has to be laden with unexpected attributes. (3) Comes with a "concerned personal touch." (4) Customers feel "significantly important." (5) Demonstrates authenticity. (6) Switches on an opportunity for further transaction. In addition to creative ideas what is importantly necessitated is perceptiveness about the customer and his use. The wheels in the chair could be made dust proof with a special chemical coating, for instance, without the customer knowing it. The more conversant the supplier and his team is, about the customer and his purpose, the more the customer delight.

3. *Realizing need of internal supplier and internal customer.* The conceptual clarity in its most chaste form about internal customer and internal supplier has yet to settle into industry and those who run it. However, it is being talked about rampantly wherever efforts to enhance productivity is being realized. If an operative is not perceptive about the doings of his "supplier" he would tend to overlook the pace, the quantity and the parameters of what he is receiving and carry out his bit of operations by overcoming the constraints that could have been well done with much more ease by his "supplier"; or the other option he would have is to increase rejection to assure quality. In many factories where both empathy and

perceptiveness have been sidelined in the work culture, such rejec-
tions are rampant, only to add to the woes of the manufacturer in
terms of rework cost and overall productivity. The internal customer
and internal supplier concept does not pertain only to operations.
This is equally vital in interdepartmental or cross domain communication or transactions as well; and even to staff functions. Most of
the failures noticed in HR roles of not having "enough knowledge"
about operations, emanate from this. It becomes more noticeable
in HR roles because human issues reflect in behavior proliferating
in huge propensities, not that Finance has any less failures when
costing issues are not comprehended in the perspective of actual
supply chain or for that matter the product management team is
not catching up with the issues raised by the product development
team or vice versa. The fundamental issue is lack of perceptiveness.
If I, working in Finance, am thorough with the ground realities of
the supply chain and not just referring to the flow chart, I would
not raise objections to insignificant material loss while transporting
it from the yard to the hopper if I am aware of (perceptive to) inevitable spillage because of the trolleys used, even though I am not an
operations person. I would also eventually empathize more with the
problem. My "suppliers" would be (1) the loader of the raw material
into the trolleys and (2) the receiver at the hopper who would be
providing the data that I would corroborate for my "perceptive"
costing. This takes me back to an incident where I was involved
as a waste management consultant. The company was set out to
erect and commission its state of the art motorcycle plant and was
successfully manufacturing its scooters. However, since a large scale
transfer from the scooter plant was contemplated, the operatives
were made to undergo stringent mindset changes in terms of waste
management. Approach changes were what the management was
looking for. One of the glaring offenders was an operator who overlooked the spillage of coolants and other oils from his machine that
flowed into the operational space of another operator compelling
him to stack his finished material in a not so easily accessible space
thereby disarming his "customer" of his efficiency and productivity
in the long run. So much for the perceptiveness of the offender.

I am saying this because all operatives were trained in 5S and its use on the shop-floor. On the contrary I had noticed an edible oil manufacturing company focusing entirely on housekeeping knowing its effects on productivity. Although the operatives hailed from the hinterland with almost a rural background, they expressed their anguish and raised an alarm if any "supplier" was off the mark. All that the company excelled in was benchmarking with the best; the operatives were taken around to other cities and industrial areas, whenever the annual shut down happened. This worked out miracles and made them see beyond.

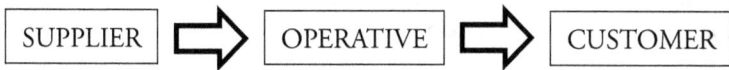

| SUPPLIER | ⇨ | OPERATIVE | ⇨ | CUSTOMER |

Role of Perceptiveness in Junior Management or Supervisory Functions

Now who is really a supervisor? A person, who knows the operations to the tee, has excellent insight to the "connect" between the tasks performed and possessing outstanding interpersonal abilities to be able to make the most of the existing resources. This inevitably requires effective and assertive communication, ability to resolve conflicts and solve problems, critical thinking, prioritizing abilities, ability to address generational and cultural diversities and above all perceptiveness on a grand scale. The last one becomes the driving force for sharpening the others mentioned. With today's developments—emerging channels, the proliferation of social media and the mobile, the competitive importance of customer relationships, and the wide range of generations our customers represent, only to name a few—supervisors have become increasingly important, contrary to the prediction of experts just a few years ago when it was assumed that technology would almost replace them. Human understanding has no substitute so far.

The table here shows the similarities in supervisory roles, whether the supervisors be on the shop-floor or managing a sales team. The premise here, which I am going by, is that all supervisors have a great deal of commonalities in their roles. The two-way arrows in the table are pointing at them. Let us examine each one of them one by one.

Role of supervisor in manufacturing operations	Role of supervisor in selling
Enforce safety and sanitation regulations	Confer with company officials to develop methods and procedures to increase sales, expand markets, and promote business
Direct and coordinate the activities of employees engaged in the production or processing of goods, such as inspectors, machine setters, and fabricators	Listen to and resolve customer complaints regarding services, products, or personnel
Confer with other supervisors to coordinate operations and activities within or between departments	Provide staff with assistance in performing difficult or complicated duties
Plan and establish work schedules, assignments, and production sequences to meet production goals	Monitor sales staff performance to ensure that goals are met
Inspect materials, products, or equipment to detect defects or malfunctions	Formulate pricing policies on merchandise according to profitability requirements

1. **Conferring with colleagues and seniors including those from other domains or shops.** The abilities needed here are
   (a) Yearning to know the others' perspective about a common issue
   (b) Explain and express the problems/issues candidly and with clarity—in other words with confident communicating ability
   (c) Arrive at an understanding that is closest to reality (being pragmatic)
   (d) Arrive at a consensus to strategize and address the issue
   (e) Interpersonal ability
2. **Direct and coordinate the activities of employees engaged in the production or processing of goods, such as inspectors, machine setters, and fabricators.** The abilities needed are
   (a) Yearning to complete task on time
   (b) Yearning to ensure that all parameters of dimensions, constituents, shape, and size match to the tee
   (c) Interpersonal ability
   (d) Ability to maintain the rhythm of production at each workstation consistently
   (e) Ability to track inputs required at each station
3. **Inspect materials, products, or equipment to detect defects or malfunctions.** Abilities required are

(a) Eye for detail to observe deviations from norms

(b) Analytical ability

(c) Ability to be proactive to restore normalcy and sustain supplies

4. Formulate pricing policies on merchandise according to profitability requirements

(a) Planning ability

(b) Ability to be aware about the market: product price/product design/competition

(c) Ability to foresee

(d) Ability to communicate logically/assertively

What is found to be common amongst all these abilities or competencies listed?

Competencies are usually further split into its constituents to observe them, make them measurable, relate them to the workplaces to ensure their context and also transfer them. Here, spring out the significance of behavioral indicators.

Let us create a table for each of the competencies listed earlier along with their behavioral indicators that we normally would identify.

Sl. no.	Competency or ability	Behavioral indicator
1	Yearning to know the other's perspective	• Assume that others may see things that you may have missed* • Consider your point of view open to change
2	Confident and clear communicating ability	• A stable and clear voice tone • Making eye contact • Listening to others* • Not attacking or threatening • Acknowledging others*
3	Being pragmatic	• Fact oriented • Coherent and logical • Alert to situation and environment*
4	Problem solving approach	• Take action without being asked • Go beyond traditional approaches* • Devise ways to overcome obstacles-resourceful • Use logic and critical thinking to analyze • Persistent* • Focus is on getting desired outcome

5	Interpersonal ability	• Build mutual respect, fairness and equity • Understand perspectives of others and demonstrates empathy* • Respect for people and their differences • Creates opportunities for inclusion in a variety of settings • Promotes and sustains a platform that acknowledges and celebrates differences
6	Completing tasks on time/meeting deadlines	• Recognizes the relative importance of certain tasks and responsibilities and has the ability to prioritize to ensure that deadlines are met • Actively demonstrates commitment by maintaining a consistent and predictable work schedule • Is relied upon by others as a source for valid information*
7	Finishing to the tee/perfection	• Exhibition of an aspiration not likely to be achieved but the pursuit of which creates a mindset and culture of continuous improvement • Accepting/realizing that what one sees is possible is only limited by the paradigms through which one sees and understands the world*
8	Consistency	• Building strong will power • Being regular • Walking the talk • Eliminating negative approach • Building habits*
9	Alertness (*Depends on both psychological and physiological factors*)	• Paying close and continuous attention • Being watchful and prompt to meet danger and emergency* • Being quick to see through and act*
10	Eye for detail	• Provides accurate, consistent numbers on all paperwork • Provides information on a timely basis and in a usable form to others who need to act on it* • Maintains a checklist, schedule, calendar, and so on to ensure that small details are not overlooked • Carefully monitors the details and quality of own and others' work* • Expresses concern that things be done right, thoroughly, or precisely • Takes necessary actions to produce work that requires little or no checking

11	Analytical ability	• Undertakes complex tasks and breaks them down into manageable parts in a systematic way • Thinks of multiple possible causes and anticipates consequences of situations* • Thinks of possible alternatives for a situation • Recognizes and reconciles data discrepancies • Identifies information needed to effectively solve problems* • Weighs the pros and cons of options and alternatives* • Systematically changes variables to determine effects on the whole, and so on
12	Proactive	• Solution focused* • Accountable* • Honest • Seeks advice (when required) • Utilizes strength complementarily • Plans action
13	Planning ability (*actually a blend of many other competencies or abilities*)	• Studying current situation and environment* • Creating a roadmap that would fit the groove • Putting first things first • Involving people for implementation* • Evaluating constantly*

The observation in the preceding table, leads us to identify the commonalities in the behavior. I have attempted to mark them with an asterisk. The intention is to discover, as to what is that common force or forces that inspire and prompt us to "pick" a behavioral pattern; and *not* to find the similarities in behavior. Let us aggregate these behaviors to try and read that stimuli within.

- Assume that others may see things that you may have missed[1]
- Listening to others[1]
- Acknowledging others[1]
- Alert to situation and environment[2]
- Go beyond traditional approaches[3]
- Persistent[4]
- Understand perspectives of others and demonstrates empathy[1]

- Is relied upon by others as a source for valid information[1/5]
- Accepting/realizing that what one sees is possible is only limited by the paradigms through which one sees and understands the world[3]
- Building habits[4]
- Being watchful and prompt to meet danger and emergency[2]
- Being quick to see through and act[2]
- Provides information on a timely basis and in a usable form to others who need to act on it[1/5]
- Carefully monitors the details and quality of own and others' work[1]
- Thinks of multiple possible causes and anticipates consequences of situations[2]
- Identifies information needed to effectively solve problems[5]
- Weighs the pros and cons of options and alternatives[3]
- Solution focused[4]
- Accountable[4]
- Studying current situation and environment[1]
- Involving people for implementation[1]
- Evaluating constantly[3]

Clubbing of those behaviors have been attempted which upfront appears to get espoused by certain attributes that describe the person. Here is finally a point wise narrative of a "perceptive" supervisor—perceptive because of his consistent social awareness and alertness. (Udai Pareek)

1. Others-oriented (higher sociability)
2. Vigilant and observant (higher alertness)
3. Resilience (flexibility)
4. Relentlessly engaged (persistently focused)
5. Information oriented (conforming to data)

Role of Perceptiveness in Managerial and Leadership Responsibilities

Since we are now embarking an arena where contributions have been observed to be unending and sometimes even repeats, without any intended plagiarism, I might as well caution the readers that finer distinctions have to be comprehended in their proper perspectives. I have been coming across articles in recent times about how people with higher sensitivity could become better managers. Most of the derivations are based on the phenomenal work Dr. Elaine Aron has put in, on the subject of sensitivity. However, let me clarify by making out a difference between what is being highlighted through this work and what has been cited by Dr. Elaine Aron in her book "The Highly Sensitive Person." While she has projected demeanors of greater sensitivity of people and has made an attempt to nullify (through techniques suggested) the downturn effects of such behavior and convert them toward a positive contribution, the endeavor in this work is to look at people with a higher resource to information and higher alertness to developments around them; who might as well possess such sensitivity but the latter is well within one's emotional and social control and has no downturn effects. The stark dissimilarity is that sensitivity is an emotional arousal, whereas perceptiveness is an innate ability for which the mind needs to get trained.

Gerard F. Becker and Jane Saber reckoned "perceptiveness" in their work for the first time in the management world—*Leadership, social perceptiveness and strategic planning in the small business environment: an evolving leadership requirement for the 21st century (2007)*. The paper spoke about the perceptiveness required by a leader for all the stakeholders of the business he was leading. However, Becker and Saber had made their contribution based on research carried out by prominent behavioral scientists and strategy experts such as Mumford, Mintzberg, Leiberman, Porter and the like. In other words, they had very carefully built on the plinth for which the foundation was laid out already, but creditably revealed the most crucial tool for a leader /manager today—perceptiveness. They have based their understanding of perceptiveness in the light of social perceptiveness which has been defined as follows by Mumford, Zaccaro, Harding, Jacobs, and Fleischman (2000)—...an ability to acclimate to various requirements for different stakeholders, internal and external to the organization. Therefore, this contribution has been based primarily in the organizational/leadership context.

The effort in this book, on the other hand, is a narrative on a more generic ability of any individual and underlines the application of that ability in various vocations, as we have seen in earlier chapters. Since, here, we are trying to discover its application in leadership and management, the descriptions of aligned contributions have been cited.

Let us now turn to fundamental concepts on types of leadership, viz., transactional and transformational. The concept of transformational leadership was initially introduced by leadership expert, historian and presidential biographer James MacGregor Burns [1918–2014].[6] Burns distinguished between transactional leaders and those who were transformational, thus:

1. Transactional leaders were those, who exchanged tangible rewards for the work and loyalty of followers.
2. Transformational leaders were those, who engaged with followers, focused on higher order intrinsic needs, and raise consciousness about the significance of specific outcomes and new ways in which those outcomes could be achieved.

In today's world we need to concentrate more on the transformational types, as change is significantly rapid and organizations must cope with the changing expectations of all the stakeholders, within and without, to successfully sustain competition. This is a universal factor in today's context. Therefore, transformational leadership is more contextual. In one of my blogs www.peoplemattertome.blogspot.com I had stopped by, to upload an approach, I had observed earlier, on the subject of leadership "differently" and had titled it as: Leadership—A Process (2002), wherein the endeavor was to examine the concept from a perspective of changing and evolutionary times that the management world was subjected to; and what leadership needed to do to cope for survival. The different stages of the spiral climb to achieve success had been laid out as:

- Learn—concepts, discoveries, events/happenings that make an impact, people, regulations
- Evaluate—what is relevant, what has a distant impact and that have none

---

[6] Leadership by James MacGregor Burns published by Harper & Row (1978).

- Assimilate—convert the information base into a repository of knowledge
- Demonstrate—walk the talk
- Empathize—realize what can be implanted amongst followers and simplify, if it can be
- Recognize—those who are able to catch on and showcase them
- Sharpen—provide space to hone up newly acquired knowledge into implementable skills
- Heighten—offer opportunities to tweak and improve qualitatively as a team
- Innovate—implement the new norms to conform to the changed group approach
- Perform—show it off in organizational action, reflecting them in figures, data and publicity

Now, if we examine Burns' behavioral indicators of a transformational leader, they would be more easily comprehensible and in sync with what we are trying to explain simplistically as a process.

- Leadership is proactive
- Works to change the organizational culture by implementing new ideas
- Employees achieve objectives through higher ideals and moral values
- Motivates followers by encouraging them to put group interests first
- Individualized consideration: Each kind of behavior is directed to each individual to express consideration and support
- Intellectual stimulation: Promote creative and innovative ideas to solve problems

It would be still easier to understand the role of a transformational leader, if we examine the path that he or she has to follow, starting from *learning*. What is it that the proactive[i] leader has to learn? It is imperative that the leader has to inevitably keep learning; else how would the new ideas ever be brought in? He or she has to earmark with updates that are relevant to his or her vertical or domain. This information would either be sourced from inside the organization or more likely from outside. The eyes and ears have to be open. Perceptiveness, as you see, plays a very significant role here, both in identifying the information itself and how it could be sourced in full. This will also help building a learning culture in the organization.

Moving on to the next step in the process, is *evaluating* the information for extracting its relevance to the organization. There are a few questions one would ask while evaluating the information. What is the authenticity of the information? Is the information objective or is it based on biases? What is the source? How contemporary or timely is the information? Is the information validated or one has to do so? Finding answers to these questions the leader has to go beyond his normal pattern of work and extend his reach in a number of ways. What is it that would lead him through this research, next to being proactive? The most palpable response would be perceptiveness. The eyes and ears would have to be open to not only data that is received as a direct inflow, but also grab those that tend to traverse a by-lane in the milieu of communication channels, one comes across while researching.

Assimilating information is a skill that the leader has to adapt to as the next step in the process. The mind has to be trained to retain as much as possible, at the risk of even being called a nerd, so that the repository is created. Michel Koopman, the CEO of get Abstract, a global online media company that tracks down business books into 10-min summaries, says, "There is so much information…we don't know where to find things and we don't always get it in a way we want to consume it…the person or company needs to balance focus with need to find/be distracted by good ideas." Koopman says that these side conversations were necessary to foster continuous innovation (through newer ideas) and therefore, the need to add on to the repository. How else would one be able to do that, except by using one's perceptiveness? Use of the information gathered in whatever form, even if simply shared, leaves an impact on the mind and moves one step closer to becoming knowledge. The instituting of "Knowledge Circles" in organizations is one such tool that would harbor the practice of conversion of information into knowledge. All members periodically share in the forum what they have learnt new, during the intervening period, since the last meeting of the Circle was held. The discussions that follow assist in discovering the relevance and utility while nonetheless the repository gets augmented. Perceptive persons would make the best of it.

Having evaluated and assimilated the information, the benchmarks are modeled, setting the stage to *demonstrate*—to walk the talk. What matters most, is how alert and aware is the leader about the team members, their knowledge and skill background, the work culture they have gotten used to and the dreams they cherish. One's social awareness, within, is as important or significant as his awareness of the outside world. This is the first step in the process, where the interventions, actually begin. Till now, whatever was occurring resulted in a churning and a tumult that was agitating the personality of the leader as an individual, but not his work environment. When the leader has to demonstrate he has an audience to address, which is why the receptivity of the audience has to be gauged in terms of the combination of factors cited in the beginning of this paragraph, the timing and the socioeconomic environment. However pressing the need be to change the organizational culture by implementing new ideas[ii], the leader would be constrained not to proceed, till the previous factors are compatible. Perceptiveness would pre-empt either a total washout or leaving a feeble impact or sufficiently motivating. A perceptive leader would not waste valuable organizational moments on situations of nonreceptivity and would rather wait till most of the factors were found to be conducive. Perhaps it would call for a presentation in a lucid and comprehensible style to begin with, followed by one to ones on methods of running the new idea, while apprehending the challenges and how they could be overcome. When one is talking about demonstration, one would only mean a trial run. The organizational preparedness for undertaking the trial run or the pilot as many call it, has to be well planned as a team. Feedback and post feedback discussions are inevitable for understanding the unanticipated glitches and for restrategizing. The percentage of glitches would reveal the lack of perceptiveness of the leader—the more the gaps, the lesser the perceptiveness.

In our third step in the process, that is *empathizing* let us examine how employees achieve objectives through higher ideals and moral values.

Psychology Today© defines it as follows: Empathy is the experience of understanding another person's condition from their perspective. You place yourself in their shoes and feel what they are feeling. Empathy is known to increase pro-social (helping) behaviors. If we recall our introductory chapter, "Trying to define perceptiveness," it has been stated already that researchers on leadership have till now focused on empathy and direction, more than perceptiveness. This is evident from the number of publications and literature available on both the former subjects. While referring to that chapter let me also remind that these three prominent attributes had been identified as the inevitable ones in any effective leader. Not to undermine any one of them let me confess that each one is not only as important as the other but also are interdependent too. Perceptiveness inspires direction, which, in the previous paragraphs we have been discussing and viewing in a different frame (benchmarking and modeling). Direction in turn coupled with perceptiveness compels you to build empathy to take things forward through effective relationships. Empathy quietly pushes you to magnify your insight and perceptiveness about your own team, as you go along. As a second step in actual interventions the leader is in a better off place, if the empathy with the team is profound. To run the pilot would be like running a knife through butter, because you have involved and consulted your team in the action plan before positioning your action. The number of gaps or deviations would be incredibly lower. Sometimes we also assign the term "teamwork" to achievements of this kind, without comprehending the mechanics of it. The higher ideals and moral values are an outcome.

The success of the new order would admissibly be to the extent, the team is kept motivated to persist and pursue. While empathizing unfurls the gateway to receptivity and acceptability, the team mates need to be charged with commendation for achievements however small they are. This is *recognition* of their contributions toward achieving the organizational goals, set by the leader, who motivates followers by encouraging them to put group interests first, at the same time. This is a very sensitive situation and may ignite a misfire, if the balance is ignored—notwithstanding the strength of the communication made with the team. Recognition of achievements is likely to be a continuous process and may call for rewards in kind or monetary terms. Even a pat on the back or a small letter of appreciation could act as strong instruments of recognition. Sometimes even an interaction with the leader may be seen as an opportunity of recognition. The latter is a means of upholding the efforts made and ensuring their continuity toward achieving the set goals. But perceptiveness plays a significant role for the leader to assess, if the continuity was maintained and for finding out as to what measures would be necessary to channelize the deviations, if any. More the perceptiveness, more effective would be the monitoring exercised and more even-handed would be the team motivation needed.

The onus of the leader is to ensure that all the skills required for having the new order instituted, are evolved. It is a gargantuan task. First of all, all the knowledge elements have to be broken down into their doable factors. Here's an example of what it is. The Vendor Development Manager in an automotive industry needs to know that the use of refractory ceramic fiber (RCF) has recently been affected by strict regulations, forcing companies to find alternative insulation materials, especially for use as mould wraps. He has to, not only narrow down on a cost-effective substitute (in coordination with his product development team) for use in investment casting to manufacture specialized metal components, but also equip his team to comprehend the technical features of such a substitute and its applicability and efficiency. There are a number of actionable tasks that the team has to undertake. In case the management decision is to use high temperature insulating wool as a substitute, the task would entail a responsibility of (1) identifying vendors (2) validating them in terms of quality (constituent material) and cost (3) assessing the reliability of their supplies on time and (4) adaptability to design and shape. Each of these tasks would require essential skills to deploy, apart from the knowledge of HTIW. For instance, the vendor development team may have to use the skills of assessing the plant and machinery of the vendor and also his operational capabilities. First of all an individual attention would have to be systematized for each team mate. Repeated practice of the actionable task adds to the skill of doing it. This is where individual attention would be needed to *sharpen* the skills and this is exactly what Burns refers to as, individualized consideration: each kind of behavior is directed to each individual to express consideration and support[v]. The leader through his perceptiveness would generate the precise approach or strategy of founding the implementation exercise and express them freely through his colleagues and teammates in meetings, training sessions, conferences, briefing sessions and other forums. His perceptiveness would enable him to foresee the challenges; for instance with the example seen earlier, we see upgrading the knowledge of the vendor development team as a major challenge and a few ways of overcoming them would perhaps be through training or even organizing visits to other users of HTIW. The accurate solution should not belie the precision of perceptiveness.

Once the skills are honed, there would be discoveries and findings of the team mates, as they go along, which could emerge as areas of improvement, where deliverables could be qualitatively upgraded through minor alterations in the methods or the approaches. We are referring to the next stage—*heighten* the new order. Using Quality Circles or Kaizen could be the more organized forms of tweaking, besides the routine incessant feedback discussions on lacunae and gaps that have been observed while implementing and that need attention. Burns points this out as the "Intellectual stimulation[vi] that promotes creative and innovative ideas to solve problems." The most significant point that should be driven home at this juncture is about building the culture of perceptiveness in the organization. Perceptiveness should not remain a prerogative of the leader alone, while simply agreeing that it is an attribute that flows out of the leader who is the fountainhead. It is only this attribute, which would help the team mates to make the "discoveries," down the line. The suggestions would emerge out of these "discoveries" that the implementers make, which keep staring at them in the form of gaps. Now the accuracy with which these "discoveries" are made, is directly proportional to the perceptiveness the implementers behold. All possible tools in culture building[7] should possibly be used to whet the feature—training, coaching, recognition and frequent tours and trips that bring about a new exposé. Whipping up perceptiveness as an organization culture would reap huge advantages for the organization for its remaining ahead, in this era of competition.

I have in the earlier paragraphs tried to cite how contextual the transformational steps were, in the background of what Burns had promulgated

---

[7] Such culture building interventions are available at www.percontsi.com

as behavioral indicators of transformational leadership and also have sought to highlight the parity between them. The indicators have been marked with superscripts i through vi. I have not stopped short at this and have attempted to describe the process further, in order to, not only tie the loose ends, but also reveal the inevitable and unending relevance of perceptiveness that continues in this process of induced transformational leadership.

Having assured the quality of the revised system and approach, the organization matures into implementing what was being run as a pilot or a trial run. The *innovation* in the organization begins. To clarify, innovation here is being referred to the *act* of innovating and instituting change and not simply to the *idea*. Implementing the method changes and practicing the changed approach or mindset commands, is the stage that is being examined here. The mechanism to do so is preparing checklists of dos and don'ts and complying with them till they develop into a habit. The participation of the team is at the optimum and does not take a dip, because all team mates have all along and continually been involved since the initiation of the interventions—"to involve is to evolve" is the cardinal principle the leader has to abide by. To make the implementation foolproof it is crucial that before calling off the pilot run, sufficient number of audits is carried out. Perceptiveness has to flow in at every step to gauge things and assess if they were in order. The auditors' remarks or comments should be taken as value added suggestions in the process. Each performer has to measure his own performance, his internal supplier's and his internal customer's. Such a measurement would be necessitated to ensure smooth flow of goods/products or services. Perceptiveness is the key to understanding that measure. When the internal supplier is unable to supply on time, or the inputs are found in inadequate quantities or are having deviant dimensions or texture the recipient receives signals of the fact that "everything was not right" at his supplier's end. He has two options—one, he would try and salvage his colleague supplier from the problems the latter was confronting, or would escalate the issue, if it amounted to stretching his role beyond permissible limits—in both, his perceptiveness has to be in full play. This also applies to those who are front-ending and are supposed to address the customer interface. They would be better poised if they read through customer behavior well in advance—I am not talking about premonitions—they not only could well be, but also actually are, the perceptive signals the front ender receives. Every moment and in every role, therefore, perceptiveness ploughs its way to refine the quality of implementation.

As behavioral preachers, we keep claiming that the attitude of "we have achieved" always sets in complacence. Our lesson here is that more successfully the transformational leadership implements the changes, the more the deliverables shall speak about them. But with the state of competition being what it is today, should an organization rely only on its deliverables to speak to the world about the improved performance? *Perform* and create a visibility of the achievements. Visibility is therefore an important factor that re-emphasizes whatever accounts for the improved performance and by whatever means—the world ought to know, what you have done! Showcase your achievements through social media, conferences, seminars, public forums, journals and periodicals. If the world does not know your performance, your work remains unknown and therefore you are not inspired for the next change. The attitude of "we've achieved" should not go waste...behavioral preachers must review their earlier stance. The leader and the team should deploy all means to identify where and what platforms need visibility and work on them for competitive advantage. Perceptiveness is the basic tool that would provide the clue, before undertaking any massive survey or studies. Else one would

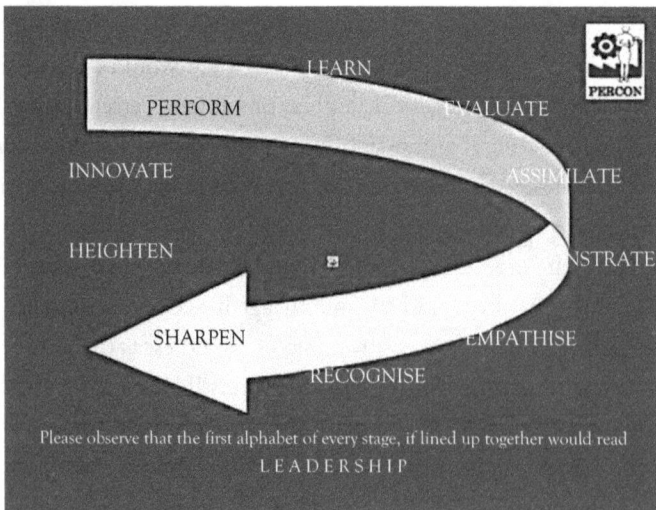

Please observe that the first alphabet of every stage, if lined up together would read
LEADERSHIP

have to address a gigantic database resource. Perceptiveness thus reduces your costs as you put your fingers on the right market segments—hence builds your corporate brand.

We have seen in the preceding paragraphs how perceptiveness assists the transformational leader and the team at every stage of the process in the makeover of an organization. Incidentally, this is not the end of its assistance. It keeps working on how and what would be the next benchmark that needs to be created—a static organization is actually vying for an early funeral.

We have seen in this chapter as to how perceptiveness works for any organization in different strata and therefore is an attribute of management studies that cannot be lost sight of. Organizations should be dedicated to build a culture of perceptiveness within, so that they stay ahead in the race. Leaders are required to feel more responsive to this need and also take on the responsibility of constructing the bridges so as to streamline the process of positioning perceptiveness as a "way of life" for each individual, each team and every working pattern. If there is a casual approach, the likelihood of getting sucked into history is obviously more. We have recently seen the decision to shut down operations by General Motors in India. The world's largest retailer Walmart said in January 2017, that it was closing 269 stores around the world. Nokia's market presence had suffered all due to the absence of the perceptiveness toward the thwarting innovation that competitors had pushed themselves, into. Medical tech firm Agilent Technologies dropped off the *Fortune* 500 this year after dropping 200 spots. And the list goes on. Michael Porter talks about competitive advantage being attained through repositioning your product or services by adding value. Dave Ulrich highlights its attainment through equipped human resources on a sustainable basis through value proposition. But how would value be added or proposed without widening the bandwidth of information and protracting it into sustainable knowledge? The conclusion is that both these would not be possible without organizational perceptiveness which is but a culmination or convergence of individual, team and leadership perceptiveness, synchronized for attaining goals and objectives.

The Future

We are walking into an era where a dignified survival would solely depend on two dimensions of working—innovative technologies and innovative strategies. Alvin Toffler in his "The Future Shock" says,

Technology makes more technology possible, as we can see if we look for a moment at the process of innovation. Technological innovation consists of three stages, linked together into a self-reinforcing cycle. First, there is the creative, feasible idea. Second, it's practical application. Third, it's diffusion through society. The process is completed, the loop closed, when the diffusion of technology embodying the new idea, in turn, helps generate new creative ideas. Today there is evidence that the time between each of the steps in this cycle has been shortened.

Shortened? Much shortened…before you can say Jack Robinson, you find there's a new software program platform! To keep pace with contemporary technology, software engineers are quitting jobs. Strangely enough, but viewing it closely, it is observed, that the quest for learning and remaining abreast with current times, overtakes the yearning to earn more. Technological innovation is need based but is directed more toward ease of operations and friendly deliverables. Involvement of the organization is necessary but is a subsequent concern.

Coming to innovative strategies let us examine the following statements and relate them to reality. Founded at Chicago, in 1966, the World Future Society is a body that helps bringing the "architects" of the future on a common platform and makes an endeavor to elicit the futurist in everyone. Director Julie Friedman Steele says that futurists tend to be "free-thinking," have a "growth mindset" and be "lifelong learners," also that "everyone is a futurist inside." Just as technology, strategies too need to get devised and revised at intervals, the expanding or shortening of which period depends on what is needed at a point in time. Unlike technological innovation, strategies can be innovated only after the involvement of the entire organization. Therefore, Steele is most apt in suggesting, what she has, to anchor well into the culture of a futuristic organization. Also, strategies cannot switch into a different mode with a blink of an eye.

It would augur well for all of us to know that Volkswagen AG has announced its "Strategy 2025," the main emphasis of which is to push for electric vehicles, which are quite a rage these days. Growing environmental consciousness and alarming pollution levels have fuelled such concerns. Volkswagen's leap into new technologies under strategy 2025 is expected to warrant investments in the double-digit billion range. However, cost-cutting at this passenger car brand outfit, bundled together with that of the company's fragmented parts operations, and realignment of its massive 12-brand business, should assist Volkswagen to finance its long-term goals. The German auto giant had set aside €16.2 billion ($18.4 billion) in terms of penalty if any that would arise related to the emissions scandal that shot it into negative prominence in 2015. Eventually Volkswagen had to pay $4.3 billion earlier this year (2017) as fine to the U.S. Courts where it was sued for by-passing U.S. pollution norms. Emphasis on cleaner technologies bodes well for Volkswagen, because this could be where the automotive growth is heading. I observe two planes on which the leadership of the auto major deployed its perceptiveness here, looking at the future circumstances. (1) Building a safeguard ploy for damage control in terms of its reputation and brand, which was twofold—(a) accepting and not refuting the scandal allegations [this becomes evident from the following facts: Judge Sean Cox, who called the cheating "a case of deliberate and massive fraud," assigned Larry Thompson to be an independent monitor to oversee VW for a probationary period of three years. Hiltrud Werner, VW's head of integrity and legal affairs, welcomed the appointment of Mr. Thompson and said the carmaker had already "taken significant steps to strengthen accountability, enhance transparency and build a better company"] and (b) budgeting for the fines or penalty, well in advance, rather than having to stroke an imbalance in the budgetary provisions later. And (2) taking advantage of the subject "environmental friendliness" for which VW had been defamed into notoriety and building from there. Converting such defamation into a positive image was no ordinary feat. But the perceptiveness to build a strategy around it was even more remarkable. VW is bidding to take a position in the environment friendly market by beating out Tesla, the largest electric car manufacturer.

Toronto-based Four Seasons is another great example of a brand that put in time, over the years to develop very detailed standards, practices and training. This has been able to help Four Seasons grow fairly quickly as a brand, while retaining its reputation for excellence in the hospitality vertical. The philosophy, guiding the management, can be seen in the following few lines that I have adapted from their website,

Times change, but our dedication to perfecting the travel experience never will. Our highly personalized 24-hour service, combined with authentic, elegant surroundings of the highest quality, embodies a home away from home for those who know and appreciate the best. As the company has grown from a single hotel to 105 in 43 countries, our deeply instilled culture, personified by our employees, continues to get stronger. Over more than 50 years, our people have built an unrivalled depth of reliability, trust and connection with our guests—a connection we will steadfastly uphold, now and always.

The perceptiveness culture has been well ingrained, because of which brands such as these are never asleep at the switch and are consistently improving. Among the 18 new 5-star rankings awarded to existing hotels worldwide this year (2017), Rosewood snagged three, Four Seasons, Ritz-Carlton and Mandarin earned two each, and Park Hyatt added one to its portfolio. The expansion of the Four Seasons business has been gigantic and has moved with times and location. Some of them may sound quite queer, but they have emerged as reality. They have diversified into air travel by providing private jet plane services, a value add to dimensions in tourism across the world. Envisioning this was no ordinary step and was not possible without an intense order of perceptiveness. Four Seasons have also invested into reality business with luxury residences in a country like India in its NCR or the National Capital Region, where infrastructure and housing is the need of the hour. This group surely is visioning futuristically. Like all businesses Four Seasons had to come across challenging times but the perceptiveness and ethical standards of the group kept it sailing through. Just to quote Chris Hart Four Seasons Hotels and Resorts Asia Pacific Hotel Operation President (2013)

> Four Seasons already has one operational hotel in Mumbai and is looking to add two more to its kitty in Bangalore and Goa. We have been looking at India for a long time. We have one property under construction at Bangalore, one in Delhi-NCR and the third one is in planning and development stage in Goa. So, we now are looking at four tangible projects in India.

Let me not highlight the personal growth of Sunil Bharti Mittal and make it sound synonymous with the growth of the now telecom giant—Airtel, although it would be difficult to segregate the two. Sunil Bharti Mittal is the son of an erstwhile renowned politician from Ludhiana in Punjab, but his growth was not pursuant of that fact. The entire credit goes to his zeal and his being perceptive to opportunities that he noticed and others did not. From borrowing Rupees 20 Thousand from his father to becoming a manufacturer of bicycle spare parts to entering the stainless steel sheet manufacture to trading in the same product in Mumbai, Sunil kept gathering the pebbles of experience of sales and finding opportunities as he went along. His perceptiveness led him to find an opportunity of selling Suzuki portable generators. He was doing well, till the biggies such as the house of the Birlas and Siddharth Shriram tied up with Yamaha and Honda respectively to launch their portable gen-sets only to chase away Sunil and his business dealing with a similar product in the Indian market. Sunil went around scouting for a new business, when he spotted push button telephones in Taiwan, and realizing its novelty in India, which was still using the rotary dialers. That is when Beetel happened with assemblies in his Ludhiana factory of semi knocked down components imported from Taiwan. Later Bharti Telecom Ltd the new-found company to manufacture these phones collaborated with Siemens AG. The company then went on to launch various telecom technologies into the Indian market and had innovation at its heart and perceptiveness in its mind. Going on to acquire license to build a cellular network in Delhi, Bharti Telecom Limited laid the ground work for the mobile operations of the company in the year 1992. It began operations in Delhi in the year 1995 as Bharti Tele-Ventures. The service was extended to various other states by various acquisitions and partnerships. Sunil Bharti Mittal rebranded all of his mobile telecom ventures under a single brand-named Airtel in 2003. Airtel is a name that connects India with millions of people all over the world *with millions of people in India.* Today, this telecom giant is amongst the most trusted telecommunication brands in the world. Its journey from a regional operator limited to the city of Delhi to second largest mobile operator in the Asia Pacific region is certainly more than inspiring. Even after the grand stroke of Mukesh Ambani's Jio, Airtel has continued its tirade in the competitive warfare by providing a facility of carrying over leftover data nonusage to the next billing cycle free of charge as accruals.

The list of such examples could be a long one, but the idea is to exemplify how companies have grown multidimensionally and retrieved from the downswings with the power-packed perceptiveness of its leadership coupled with creative strategy, which again is an outcome of data in the repository, acquired through filtered perceptiveness. Not only to remain ahead in times of turbulence but also to sustain the "market leader" positions, by updating information on market and technology innovation strategies, being perceptive has lent a big hand.

To take you back to Darwin's utilitarian theory of "struggle for existence" and "survival of the fittest," one of the most significant criteria for staying the fittest in contemporary terms, seems to be perceptiveness. The more perceptive one is, the more likely one is to remain ahead. It is a proficiency that needs to be developed by one and all, in this competitive world—whether one's needs are material, or they are spiritual (notwithstanding competition becomes meaningless in such a case, the "assimilation" would expectedly happen much faster). Let us examine the four steps that could help us, in sharpening our perceptiveness skills. (A) The mind has to be kept unbiased and open to receiving information. (B) The filters in the mind should be able actionable—twofold (1) classify the information and stack them in the repositories of the mind and (2) accept or reject according to relevance. (C) Recall the information as and when to be put to use and (D) deploy the recall cautiously, dexterously and differently for each individual, group or situation depending on the responses received or expected to be received.

The Postlude

Ignorance, elders always said was bliss
Questioning so, was what led me amiss
But hands were held, someone drove me through
Found words along the cove that near me drew
Ideas and ways of putting them together
Fell in place as it happened before, never
From titling to writing the epilogue
T 'was journeying from temple to synagogue
As every challenge was fought to end the strife
Thoughts slowly were clearer and larger than life
But could do nothing much, but collect pebbles
Till strewn were they, to trounce the rubbles
Did I do it? Nay, shall I say it was Him
The illumination that dispelled the dim
Giving expression to perceptiveness was but an excuse
Salvaged from indulgence, one amongst many rescues
Being giving and surrendering is the answer
Receiving just happens, not a hurdle nor a bouncer

References

1. Meditations by Marcus Aurelius (translated into English in 1792 by Richard Graves).
2. Training Instruments by Udai Pareek. Chapter 2. Published by McGraw Hill Education.
3. Aggarwal, J.C. 2002. *Philosophical and Sociological Perspectives on Education.* Shipra Publications.
4. Social: Why Our Brains Are Wired to Connect by Matthew D. Lieberman published by Oxford University Press.
5. *Leadership, social perceptiveness and strategic planning in the small business environment: an evolving leadership requirement for the 21st century (2007)* - Paper by Gerard F. Becker and Jane Saber
6. Leadership by James MacGregor Burns published by Harper & Row 1978.

About the Author

Dhruva Trivedy had very humble beginnings and was born to a family of artists, performing arts included. The parents were from two different cultural and language backgrounds. They were conscientious about values and tried to hand them over, as best as they could.

From schooling to post graduation he attempted to collect all the pebbles that lay on the shores of knowledge, which was streaming through his friends, teachers, elders, colleagues, and helping hands, who inspired him in more than one way.

With a postgraduation in the HR domain from the Tata Institute of Social Sciences, Mumbai, he began his quest to exploit his abilities in interpersonal relationships and build on them. He moved out of his comfort zone, first from the HR domain to Operations from the Corporate to Consulting and experimented his love for Academics by doing part-time assignments with B-Schools. But his admiration for Consulting kept him preoccupied with the throes and challenges of change.

He has been writing blogs and articles which have been published by magazines, journals, and newspaper dailies.

Amongst many other accolades that he has been receiving for his contributions, Dhruva Trivedy was adorned with the title of a "Thought Leader" by CIPD, London on the centenary celebrations of the CIPD in 2013.

About the Editor

Dr. Mohammad Tausif-ur-Rahman is a Professor at the Indira Gandhi National Tribal University, primarily engaged in English Communication training. He has designed and taught courses on writing skills for young learners at British Council ELTC. He is also the author of two books that have been published for English Language Teaching. He is also a member of Pearson India Resource Panel for Teacher Training.

Index

OTHER TITLES IN THE HUMAN RESOURCE MANAGEMENT AND ORGANIZATIONAL BEHAVIOR COLLECTION

- *Conflict First Aid: How to Stop Personality Clashes and Disputes from Damaging You or Your Organization* by Nancy Radford
- *How to Manage Your Career: The Power of Mindset in Fostering Success* by Kelly Swingler
- *Deconstructing Management Maxims, Volume I: A Critical Examination of Conventional Business Wisdom* by Kevin Wayne
- *Deconstructing Management Maxims, Volume II: A Critical Examination of Conventional Business Wisdom* by Kevin Wayne
- *The Real Me: Find and Express Your Authentic Self* by Mark Eyre
- *Across the Spectrum: What Color Are You?* by Stephen Elkins-Jarrett
- *The Human Resource Professional's Guide to Change Management: Practical Tools and Techniques to Enact Meaningful and Lasting Organizational Change* by Melanie J. Peacock
- *Tough Calls: How to Move Beyond Indecision and Good Intentions* by Linda D. Henman
- *The 360 Degree CEO: Generating Profits While Leading and Living with Passion and Principles* by Lorraine A. Moore
- *The Concise Coaching Handbook: How to Coach Yourself and Others to Get Business Results* by Elizabeth Dickinson

Announcing the Business Expert Press Digital Library

Concise e-books business students need for classroom and research

This book can also be purchased in an e-book collection by your library as

- a one-time purchase,
- that is owned forever,
- allows for simultaneous readers,
- has no restrictions on printing, and
- can be downloaded as PDFs from within the library community.

Our digital library collections are a great solution to beat the rising cost of textbooks. E-books can be loaded into their course management systems or onto students' e-book readers. The **Business Expert Press** digital libraries are very affordable, with no obligation to buy in future years. For more information, please visit **www.businessexpertpress.com/librarians**. To set up a trial in the United States, please email **sales@businessexpertpress.com**.